My Dear Children
One Step Closer to Jesus

Tim Peterson

IHP PRACTICA

Copyright © 2025 Tim Peterson. All rights reserved. Except for brief quotations in critical publications or reviews, no part of this book may be reproduced in any manner without prior written permission from the publisher: admin@illativehousepress.com.

Paperback ISBN: 979-8-9990929-0-8

IHP PRACTICA
An Imprint of Illative House Press, LLC
500 E. Elm St.
West Frankfort, IL 62896
IllativeHousePress.com

All IHP publications are available through Amazon.com.

Cover artwork: Sebi, CC BY-SA 3.0 via Wikimedia Commons
Cover design: Illative House Press

Unless otherwise indicated, all Scripture quotations are from The Holy Bible, English Standard Version® (ESV®). © 2001 by Crossway, a publishing ministry of Good News Publishers. All rights reserved.

For the next generation.

First to my children—Kara and Micah—who were physically born to us. Then to our Uganda children—Kakuba, Mwine, John, and Segi—who God gave us to live in our home for a time. Also to our Ebenezer family children whom we loved as best as we were able.

My desire and prayer is not to write a bestseller. I want people (my children primarily) to read about God's authority, His Spirit, and His wisdom, and see His glory reflected in the pages of this book. My heart is that they be constantly pointed back to Jesus, to the Holy Spirit, and to intimacy with our Father God.

Introduction

Joy as a father.
Great joy in You, heavenly Father.
Thank You.

My Dear Children,

You have heard me say that my heart is to walk with you one step closer to Jesus. This book is a tangible reminder of things I have taught you. I want to walk with you. Will you travel with me for a little while down this path closer to Jesus? Just agreeing to walk together takes us closer to Jesus—Jesus in you for me and Jesus in me for you.

My hope is that our hearts grow in passion for intimately meeting Jesus (God with us, Immanuel) everywhere we go, in every conversation we have, in every decision we make, and in every experience we encounter.

Did you ever have a dream to accomplish something in your future but were uncertain how to get there? Maybe some barriers were in the way. Perhaps there was some doubt, some unknown mountains to climb or river to forge. Maybe the dream was a bit foggy and unclear. Did you walk a bit and find out it was actually someone else's dream you were trying to live out?

My hope is to give you some thoughts that resonate and connect with God's desire He has already put in you; the sort of dream He made you to accomplish, and you know it deeply in your heart and soul. I hope the notes the Holy Spirit sings through me will be in tune with the notes He is singing in you.

Maybe some of this will ring true to you and you will recognize that God is working the same purpose in you. You might find that you have tried what I write about, but it hasn't turned out like you expected, and you gave up. Maybe I or someone else has hurt you along your way and what I write reminds you of the pain you are trying to avoid. Maybe because of all that pain, what I say seems like a lie.

I want to say that I am deeply sorry for treating you in an ungodly way at times. I remember doing that to each of you. For myself and on behalf of others who should have cared for you truly with the love of Jesus but didn't, I'm asking you to release us into the judgment of the just and righteous God who knows all. I would love for you to be free of carrying the judgment that only God can rightly and justly carry out. Only in that type of forgiveness can you be free day after day, moment by moment.

It is in this freedom I am hoping we can walk together through the pages of this book. I hope that Jesus, who is walking with us, will point out each of the areas He has already been working on in us and encourage us as we make progress. I also hope Jesus will remind us of areas that we need His help to acknowledge and grow (which we definitely can).

All these areas we will journey through are both an ideal destination and a gift on the journey of the Christ-follower's life. Obviously there are many more themes throughout Scripture that we could focus on. For me, the ones I write about have risen to the surface. At times they have shocked and confronted me. At times, they have downright disturbed me in my complacency and negativity. But most of all, they have been a joy to see as goals and blessings to intentionally pursue.

I hope, pray, and believe that Jesus will point out to you what you need, first for your benefit but then even more. What happens in you will only be a seed planted to bear fruit for Christ's Kingdom. I am confident of that. I hope you can smile about, stop and process through, wrestle with, weep over, and long for what we discuss along our journey. I hope that on our journey in and closer to Jesus, you will recognize the character of Jesus working in you and with you. I hope the more you see Jesus in and around you on this journey, the less you will focus on yourself. Hopefully, you will be amazed that His protection, His compassion, His comfort, and His care are enough. I hope that the more you see Him, the less you need to think about yourself because He's got you.

I hope that the Bible verses I use will encourage you, convict you, clarify what you already know, show you what you need to remember, and reveal what you have never heard before. I hope these verses remind you of what you have had to change in your life. I hope you will grow in certain areas of your life and find helpful ways to receive Jesus's presence.

If you have never completely surrendered to Jesus, I hope and pray that Jesus will reveal Himself as the Good Shepherd He truly is. I pray you will come to complete surrender to your Savior, Jesus Christ, by believing what He did was for your salvation. If you haven't made that choice, the rest of this book may not make sense to you. But I pray it will plant seeds to change your eternal future. If you want to know what that looks like, skip to the Appendix at the end of the book. The way to salvation is there.

If you have made that decision affirmatively, I am confident that God will carry on to completion what He started in you (Philippians 1:6). I also hope that this is less about what you are not and more about what you were made for and designed to be. God will take you there because He is faithful. In Him we will grow to be faithful.

Let's take a walk together—*One Step Closer to Jesus.*

> "I will remind you…
> so that after my departure you may…
> recall these things." 2 Peter. 1:12,15

Chapter 1

Glory

"...to the praise of His glorious grace..." Ephesians 1:6

I think you know me well enough to know that I want my life to have purpose and meaning. Reading through Ecclesiastes, it doesn't take long to see how many ways Solomon[1] tried to find meaning. My guess is the teacher's life was mostly over and he was feeling like he came up empty in spite of his good beginning. At the end he says, "Fear God and keep his commandments, for this is the whole duty of man" (Ecclesiastes 12:13).

What a miserable feeling to know, maybe like Solomon, that you are close to the end of your life. You have wasted your life trying, and now you have come full circle, depending on the God your dad trusted, feared, and obeyed.

So if fearing God and keeping His commands are our duty, how do I—how do we—get there? That's a good question. Let's go for a walk with Moses up the mountain, the same mountain where God said:

> And you shall set limits for the people all around, saying, "Take care not to go up into the mountain or touch the edge of it. Whoever touches the mountain shall be put to death." (Exodus 19:12)

> Indeed, so terrifying was the sight that Moses said, "I tremble with fear." (Hebrews 12:21)

> For I was afraid of the anger and hot displeasure that the LORD bore against you, so that he was ready to

---

[1] There are many views on who wrote Ecclesiastes. I believe there is good evidence that Solomon is at least the logical prototype, especially as you look at the trajectory of his life from beginning to end.

> destroy you. But the LORD listened to me that time also. (Deuteronomy 9:19)

Moses kept coming back to appeal to God.

> Moses said to the LORD, "See, you say to me, 'Bring up this people,' but you have not let me know whom you will send with me. Yet you have said, 'I know you by name, and you have also found favor in my sight.' Now therefore, if I have found favor in your sight, please show me now your ways, that I may know you in order to find favor in your sight. Consider too that this nation is your people." (Exodus 33:12–13)

He moved toward God even though he was terrified, and God responded.

> And he said, "My presence will go with you, and I will give you rest." And the LORD said to Moses, "This very thing that you have spoken I will do, for you have found favor in my sight, and I know you by name." (Exodus 33:14, 17)

Then Moses does something that is beyond sense—maybe nonsense. "Moses said, 'Please show me your glory'" (Exodus 33:18). Why? I see Moses believing God *is* good even while He *is* terrifying. God is faithful even while He cannot be controlled.

Part of the reason a person avoids the glory of God is that it exposes them with their sin and their shame. "In their case the god of this world has blinded the minds of the unbelievers, to keep them from seeing the light of the gospel of the glory of Christ, who is the image of God" (2 Corinthians 4:4). At the same time, if we can receive the brightness of the glory of God, we also can experience the stunning beauty of His holiness.

Have you ever stepped out of a dark room into the full daylight and were temporarily blinded by the light? It wasn't until your eyes were adjusted that you began to take in your surroundings and become fully aware of your situation.

When I walk in darkness, I have no idea what is there for me as a blessing or as a danger. I remember traveling at night into Yosemite Valley for a retreat and not knowing in what part of the park we had arrived. When we woke up and walked out of the cabin, we were awestruck by the massive granite walls towering over us. They seemed to grow overnight because the darkness had hid their presence. When the light came, we were able to see reality as it truly was. The beauty and majesty were breathtaking. Now imagine walking around on top of that colossal cliff without light to shine on your steps. Who knows when you might step off the cliff to your death? Even if we know the cliff is there somewhere, it would be foolish to walk around without any light.

Yet we do that in our lives all the time when we don't walk in the light of the glory of God. We miss out on the breathtaking and breath-giving majesty and holiness of His glory. We also often step off cliffs without knowing they are there—to our detriment or demise. I had to decide this: Do I want to keep falling over and over, or do I want something more? Do I want to walk in the light?

If you have ever sat through the night needing rest but sleep has evaded you, then you know how glorious that first bit of light is on the horizon. Or have you ever been in need of help in the middle of the dark of night and saw a light, a glimmer of rescue? Most of us, if not all of us, would hope in that moment—hope for the sunrise, hope for the rescue. If you were able, would you take a step toward the light of rescue?

As a father, I was so excited to see my little child take a first step. They are called toddlers for a reason—teetering, wobbling, and then boom! They hit the floor, startled. But looking into their father's eyes and seeing joy, excitement, and no little amount of being well-pleased encourages them to try again. They might try again right away or wait a few months.

Our Heavenly Father is also well-pleased when we take just one step closer to our Savior, Jesus. We can see it with eyes of faith if we believe the character of God. With faith, we see His face and His eyes looking to us with longing, compassion, and love as we take a step closer to Jesus. He is already drawing us closer. "And I, when I am lifted up from the earth, will draw all people to myself" (John 12:32).

> So Jesus said to them, "The light is among you for a little while longer. Walk while you have the light, lest darkness overtake you. The one who walks in the darkness does not know where he is going." (John 12:35)

I believe that receiving His love gives Him glory because His love is displayed on our faces. In turn, His love displayed on our faces reveals God's glory at work in and through us to the people around us. "And we all, with unveiled face, beholding the glory of the Lord, are being transformed into the same image from one degree of glory to another. For this comes from the Lord who is the Spirit" (2 Corinthians 3:18).

His glory is displayed by His image through His loving character at work in us. If my focus is on myself, how horrible things are for me, how my life is not working out the way I want, how I feel I want to give up. My face is not turned to the glory of God in the face of Christ. "For God, who said, 'Let light shine out of darkness,' has shone in our hearts to give the light of the knowledge of the glory of God in the face of Jesus Christ" (2 Corinthians 4:6).

I experienced this very thing last week. I was focused on myself, and as far as I could see at that moment, everything was going wrong. I no longer was living the character of God for His glory by loving others. I couldn't. I was out for *my* glory, or these days we might say "my comfort" or "my ease."

Since the Garden of Eden, the children of God have defied the King. We have chosen to decide what is right rather than believe God and act from obedience. When I decide I know reality apart from Him, I create my own kingdom within God's kingdom. That is insurrection punishable by death. But praise Jesus, He has rescued me from my own scheme to supplant Him as King, and He did it by His own sacrifice. His rescue not only happened once for all, but I get to receive His loving redemption from my treason every moment of every day in my submission to His presence (His glory) in my life.

I see it in little ways—when I am grateful that He has me in His hands even when I feel grumpy; when I choose to believe His presence is with me and loving me even when or especially when I'm lonely; when I plan on something but it doesn't work out the way I wanted and I look for what He may be doing in the changed plans.

I see it in big ways—when I ask God for provision for one of you, my children, and someone praying with me obeys God and gives to you; when one of you tells me you were desperate for God to change you through forgiving others because you were becoming like the very people who hurt you; when a married couple each genuinely confesses his or her own sin that contributed to the marriage floundering.

In all these ways I see God's glory, and I get to submit to His rescue. I no longer have to control my situations and circumstances moment by moment. I no longer need to hold others in my mental and emotional jail for how they wronged me. I no longer have to stay self-absorbed. I can help others in need since He, my Savior, will supply my every need according to His riches in glory (Philippians 4:19).

This is my spiritual act of worship (Romans 12:1). My submission to God can be in every decision, every thought, every attitude, and every expression. "And we all, with unveiled face, beholding the glory of the Lord, are being transformed into the same image from one degree of glory to another. For this comes from the Lord who is the Spirit" (2 Corinthians 3:18).

Oh, I long to be there constantly, but my reality is that any given day can be harder than others. Yesterday I was irritated with people, circumstances, change of plans, miscommunication, and misunderstanding. I was stressed, tired, lonely, emotionally drained, and unsure of how to proceed. In the middle of it, I realized my mind wasn't on God and His heart. It was on me and what I didn't have that I thought I should have—primarily control. But by God's grace, I focused just a little on God's glory.

This morning I woke up with a similar attitude. By God's grace, my mind went to Matthew 11:28: "Come to me, all who labor and are heavy laden, and I will give you rest." I started offloading, out loud with hand motions, all the burdens I have been carrying. One by one, I named them specifically and with a physical gesture pushed them off my shoulders. In the middle of pushing, I was also grateful to God that He was taking the weight off and the outcomes away. He even lightened the load of the areas that were my responsibility. I realized these were my thank offerings. They were gifts given by God that I had taken on as mine to *own* rather than steward with His constant love and counsel. Now I was consciously giving them back. This seems to be just one small practical way to give God the glory.

At a pastors' conference about twenty years ago, Pastor Crawford Loritts preached a sermon I have not forgotten. He reminded us often throughout the sermon that "it's all about God!" I can hear his voice to this day. I have been increasingly trying to move in that direction, but it feels slippery saying that. Sure, it's all about God until I find myself manipulating it back to be all about me. I don't even realize it until I've hurt someone by my self-centeredness. This is the exact opposite of the character of God who cares for the needy, the downtrodden, the broken, and essentially anyone who needs help. It's all about God! That seems very strange to say, but He is constantly caring for others. How does that work?

After reading Isaiah 42:8—"I am the Lord; that is my name; my glory I give to no other, nor my praise to carved idols"—I saw that God doesn't give His glory or share His glory with anyone. But then in John 17:22—"The glory that you have given me I have given to them, that they may be one even as we are one"—Jesus is praying that He has glorified us who have believed the apostles' message so we can be one as He is one with His Father. How can this be? God doesn't share His glory, but now Jesus has glorified us. The only answer I have is that we can only be one if we are living in the Holy Spirit. Only the Spirit of God can make us one, so are we glorified because He is glory within us. Indeed, He is not glorifying us other than the glory of His presence, of the Holy Spirit shining on, in, and through us, uniting us so the world can see that God loves us just like He loves Jesus. "I made known to them your name, and I will continue to make it known, that the love with which you have loved me may be in them, and I in them" (John 17:26).

I am realizing that when life is about me, I am bringing glory to myself. But if I bring glory to God, I am a man of truth, and there is nothing false about me. If I glorify myself, my glory means nothing. "The one who speaks on his own authority seeks his own glory; but the one who seeks the glory of him who sent him is true, and in him there is no falsehood" (John 7:18). Only Jesus will glorify us by sending His Spirit to those who believe. By abiding in His Spirit, we bear fruit, showing ourselves to be His disciples (John 15:8).

Within days of writing this, your mom and I did something that we believe was led by God, even though it was seemingly contrary to certain popular Christian teaching and even seemingly contrary to the principles of biblical wisdom literature. At least we believe it was led by God. I guess that is always the question, right? How do we know? I guess it wouldn't be called faith if we knew. We prayed a lot about it. Maybe by the end of writing this book we will see more of God fulfilling His Word in leading us this way—or not. To your mom, it was a painful decision and very confusing. It was sort of like Abraham being told that God's promise would come through Isaac and then God telling him to sacrifice Isaac. To Abraham, that probably made no logical sense. But God worked through it. For us, although obeying by faith and moving to another continent was a step of believing God without knowing the outcome, the decision defied the principles and relied on our relationship with the Father, the Son, and the Holy Spirit—the Triune God.

Why did we do it? I believe it was for God's glory. How will He be glorified? Right now, the only way I am confident He will be glorified is that His character (His name) is so trustworthy that two people risked much—including, it appears, God's promise to them—in order to obey. As we were walking through this decision, a song ("Voice of Truth") and God's Word through a devotional took me within twenty-four hours to David and Goliath. My mind and heart caught David's reasoning that God defeated the lion and the bear that came against him, so why wouldn't God defeat a giant who was coming against God's character. God, this is for your glory.

Giving God the glory is always a step of faith because I have to believe that God is God and I am not nor ever will be. Giving Him the glory He deserves will, at times, go against safety, control, common sense, human wisdom, financial principles, family, friends, godly advice, self-interest, or laws of nature—or all of the above. There are biblical examples of all of these, but the common thread is listening to God in relationship with Him for His glory. Faith is never primarily for our benefit. It is always, first and foremost, for God's glory. And oh, by the way, we get some side benefits:

- honoring the true God and King
- added faith
- humility
- front-row seat to the God of the universe in action
- our name connected to Him
- knowing that He knows best and I don't, and that I can be okay with that
- deepening relationship with my Savior
- my obedience can express my love for Him

All these benefits could and should lead directly to gratefulness. Oh, how often I have taken credit for something I have accomplished when, in fact, God was accomplishing through me what should and ultimately will give Him glory. When I take credit for those accomplishments, I am stealing what is rightfully His. If, instead, I am grateful for His work in everything, then I receive many of the same benefits as glorifying Him in faith. Let's look at those benefits from the side of not being grateful.

- I am usurping the throne of the true God and King
- I am doubting that God is who He says He is
- I am increasing my pride in false self-sufficiency
- I close my eyes to His work and convince myself that God is holding out on me
- I turn my back on God and convince myself that I don't need Him
- I become judge over God and, in turn, everyone around me

- I convince myself that I am the only one who can save me—except from death
- I believe that only I can love myself adequately, so I become self-centered and systematically cut myself off from all true relationships, causing anger, bitterness, depression, anxiety, and fear

Gratefulness combats all those negative consequences and brings the center and focus back to God. Studies show the direct effect of gratefulness on negative consequences such as depression and anxiety. What if I didn't have to focus on myself and all the bad things I am going through? What if gratefulness, the true heartfelt understanding that I do not survive or ever get to a place of thriving without God providing, is my way out of those negative consequences?

Gratefulness seems to acknowledge what someone has done for us or given us. Or is it instead acknowledging the kindness, the goodness, and the love of the person who has given to us? If the latter is true, isn't gratefulness simply agreeing with the truth of what God's reality is? When this gratefulness has to do with God, then in my gratefulness I agree that God is kind and good and love. Hmm. That sounds like I agree with His character, like I'm telling the truth about Him. This is giving God the glory He deserves and is rightfully His.

Isn't it crazy that telling the truth is glorifying God? Do you see why the first temptation was to question *reality* (God's reality)? "Did God really say?" It's very interesting that the Pharisees seemed to connect telling the truth with giving God the glory. "So for the second time they called the man who had been blind and said to him, 'Give glory to God. We know that this man is a sinner'" (John 9:24). Earlier in the book of John, Jesus seems to say that if we seek our own glory, there is falsehood somewhere in us, but if we properly seek the glory of the One who sent us, we are people of truth with nothing false about us (John 7:18). He says a bit later in John, "Jesus answered, 'If I glorify myself, my glory is nothing. It is my Father who glorifies me, of whom you say, "He is our God"'" (John 8:54).

Telling the truth about who I am and who God is puts glory in its proper place. My purpose turns from my way and my glory to God's desire for His glory, which also results in my benefit. God's glory as my purpose is eternally focused and absolutely certain. If that is the goal of my life, then my life isn't empty; it is full of joy and meaning. That is exactly the conclusion the teacher in Ecclesiastes came back to. "The end of the matter; all has been heard. Fear God and keep his commandments, for this is the whole duty of man" (Ecclesiastes 12:13). But we have to believe it, by faith.

Chapter 2

Faith

Peace is received through faith.

In the last chapter, I said that your mom and I made a decision based on faith. As my children, you know that faith, my faith in God, His character, and who He has revealed Himself to be is bedrock, solid foundation for me. Actually, I will give you a picture of what I mean.

I see life like deep water—ocean water. You can learn to swim and try to master the waves, but eventually you will get tired or the waves will get beyond your ability, and you will need to put your foot down. What if in the midst of your exhaustion or in the stormy, crashing waves there was a rock right below you within your reach. Instead of believing the rock was a place of comfort, a place of security, and a place of rest, you kept stubbing your toe on it and getting mad at it. You might even try to swim away from it, but wherever you swim, it is there. At best, the rock was an irritant. At worst, it felt like the rock was there to mock you in your fear and exhaustion.

What if instead of getting mad at the rock, you decided to trust the rock and put your foot down. Maybe, even though you could swim, you explored the rock. You got to know the rock. How big was it? Was it more accessible in some places than in others? Was there a place on that rock where, even in the midst of the worst storm, you could put your foot down and *know* comfort, *know* security, and *know* rest? When you explored the rock more closely, you found treasures on it you never knew existed—beauty, life, even delicate life that existed because it stayed connected to the rock.

The irony is that sometimes the stormy waves pinned you to the rock and pummeled you. At that point, you had a choice to make. Do you leave the rock and try it on your own because it hurts too much to stay and get pinned between the waves and the rock? Do you find another rock that is more comfortable? Do you get away from the rock to set yourself free? Hmmm—free to not have comfort, security, and rest? Instead you get rolled over and over in the waves, desperate to catch your breath and wondering if you will, indeed, drown.

The crazy thing is that the rock is always there, always available. Do you want the rock? "But from there you will seek the LORD your God and you will find him, if you search after him with all your heart and with all your soul" (Deuteronomy 4:29). "You will seek me and find me, when you seek me with all your heart" (Jeremiah 29:13). It takes faith to depend on the rock and not on yourself.

There are a few components of faith that are important, maybe necessary. The first is humility. It may take faith to depend on the rock, but I do have to acknowledge that I am inadequate to make it by myself. I have to have the humility to understand that I need the rock in order to survive and thrive. I need help. If I don't acknowledge that, I will keep getting frustrated with God and start blaming Him for all that is wrong in my life. I had that choice two days ago. In my negative perspective that day, it seemed all the world and its agents were against me due to these:

- physical circumstances—like a weird burning spill on my arm
- emotional circumstances—like being alone all day and feeling discouraged and confused
- spiritual turmoil—like God, do you see me? Do you care?

I can try to take all the verses I know and recite them—sometimes that is helpful. I can try to think good thoughts—again, sometimes helpful. I could think "good thoughts"—ice cream or a day at the beach is different than what God has blessed me with, including His character. I can pray. That's absolutely necessary every time. Does that cast out the darkness? I don't know if the act of prayer does or if it is always God who casts out the darkness in response to our prayer. And is it a guarantee that He will every time? It doesn't seem like it from Scripture. Many more possibilities exist to help us get out of that dark cloud, but none are a guarantee. I believe we need humility no matter what. "God, You know what is happening to me right now. Give me Your presence in the midst of my dark cloud, and even if no part of me senses that You are present, I believe You are. Help my unbelief!" This is also the time I start calling for prayer reinforcements. One of the necessities in my life is having a group of people I can call or text and know they will pray for me. I believe this is one small way I can obey God's Word and humble myself. "I can't do this alone, God, and it feels like You aren't listening. Maybe You will listen to one of these other pray-ers."

When we need help of any kind, acknowledging our weakness to God and others is an act of humility. Think of a small child just learning to talk. We teach them to ask. Often in our house we said, "Use your words." As a child, or even as an adult, it takes humility to open our hearts in need in order to ask for help. We willfully put our dependence on the one who can help us.

Just in the last week, I experienced what I've been writing about, so this is very personal. I've been telling people who ask how I'm doing that I'm writing this book. I've also been telling people who ask how I'm doing that this has been the most challenging season of my life in terms of faith. God has given me a desire to grow in my faith, and I have been asking Him to do that in me. I know full well that by asking, He will lead me into a time when He will require me to believe Him even when all my sensibilities say that isn't wise. Sure enough, that is exactly what has been happening. He has called your mom and me into situations that are very unsettling and even scary. Just when it seems like we are challenged enough, more situations come that call us further into need, into a desperation that God will come through. Just yesterday, I awoke and up very early in the morning, crying out to God for some sort of answer. "If nothing else, at least meet me, good Father." It seemed He was directing me to Psalm 5. After reading it a couple times, I wrote in my prayer journal, "Thank You for giving me words of what is in my heart." Then I believe He led me to Psalm 88—the cry of my heart. I identified my cry in almost every detail of what the psalmist wrote. But Psalm 88:11 hit me the hardest and made me ask in my spirit:

> Is your steadfast love declared in the grave,
> or your faithfulness in Abaddon?

I felt my situation was dark, but others have gone through much worse. It doesn't get any worse than dying and being lost forever. Then my mind went to a cryptic verse in 1 Peter 3:18: "For Christ also suffered once for sins, the righteous for the unrighteous, that he might bring us to God, being put to death in the flesh but made alive in the spirit." Did Jesus indeed descend into the grave, into Abaddon, and shine His light even there? If so, why wouldn't He be shedding His light on me by His very presence since He said, "I will never leave you nor forsake you" (Hebrews 13:5)?

I had to choose to agree with this verse because there was a lot of bombardment that I was all alone and I had to just suffer and figure it out on my own. These lies were so powerful and repetitive that I was now crying out to God to combat the lies. It was in the midst of that battle that I landed on (was directed to) Psalm 5, Psalm 88, and 1 Peter 3:18. He was (is) shedding His light—Him, *the* Light—into my darkness, and it was a glorious light! Then, I believe, His Spirit took me to Psalm 42 that begins with the psalmist panting for God and thirsting for God. But then in verse 7, the psalmist wrote, "Deep calls to deep at the roar of your waterfalls; all your breakers and your waves have gone over me" (Psalm 42:7).

I don't see this as God's wrath, as many commentators say. I see this as God's love—the torrent, the powerful waterfall of God's love. The image that comes to mind is Murchison Falls in northwestern Uganda where an enormous volume of the Nile River funnels through a narrow canyon. What power! What an incredible torrent! How much infinitely more is God's overwhelming flood of love. Now, here is the question in all this: Do I believe it? Do I believe that in the midst of my darkness, Jesus, the image of the invisible God (Colossians 1:15), the Light of the world (John 9:5), love incarnate, is capable of shedding His light and love into my darkness just by His presence alone? And will I choose to believe it when nothing in my circumstances has apparently changed at all? Wow! He is indeed stretching my faith!

This is faith: choosing to believe what God has said about His character. That is also humility. "Now faith is the assurance of things hoped for, the conviction of things not seen" (Hebrews 11:1). Then follow snippets of those who lived by faith and were commended for it.

"These all died in faith, not having received the things promised, but having seen them and greeted them from afar, and having acknowledged that they were strangers and exiles on the earth" (Hebrews 11:13). They died in faith, implying that in this life they didn't get what was promised. But the writer of Hebrews seems to be saying they died essentially believing that if they didn't see God's promise fulfilled in their lifetimes, He would still fulfill His promises. And the author of Hebrews makes it very clear that this life is not all there is.

Think of David who prepared all the supplies to build the temple, but God told him he would not build it. Humility is essential to faith because I don't and won't see it all or understand it all, at least not before standing face to face with my Maker. I have to know that I cannot outthink, out plan, out love, or even out judge God. The only place faith can grow is in the soil of humility. "And without faith it is impossible to please him, for whoever would draw near to God must believe that he exists and that he rewards those who seek him" (Hebrews 11:6).

This is humility contained in complete agreement with God's Word—His written Word and also His living and breathing Word (Jesus). "I am the vine; you are the branches. Whoever abides in me and I in him, he it is that bears much fruit, for apart from me you can do nothing" (John 15:5), and He can do everything in me that He desires. "Now to him who is able to do far more abundantly than all that we ask or think, according to the power at work within us, to him be glory in the church and in Christ Jesus throughout all generations, forever and ever. Amen" (Ephesians 3:20–21). One humorous way of looking at it is this: We are dirt—humus. One definition is "the dark organic, nutrient-rich soil essential to the fertility of the earth." With this soil, the Gardener (John 15:1) can plant, till, water, and harvest an abundant crop. What does the humus do? It responds, yields, gives nutrients, holds the water for the plant to receive, or in stubbornness and detraction is rocky, thorny, or hard (Matthew 13:5–23).

I believe most of us, and from my standpoint especially me, have missed this attitude and this life of humility (humus) because of our lack of integrity. I *know* I can't meet the standard God requires, but I am not honest with myself. I refuse to admit to myself, let alone to God and everyone else, that I cannot figure it all out. At any given moment we might have the vague feeling that we have figured it out, but then the reality of unplanned circumstances and doubt set in. We realize that "I can't, but God can," and He will do the best through us and in us if we will respond to His prompting, nudging, whispering a little bit more—and then a little bit more.

It all starts with integrity—will I agree with God's reality, or am I going to continue to grit my teeth and survive through this life, creating my own reality? If I am truly honest with myself, I know I don't have everything together, and to some extent, I have been faking it and hoping for the best all along. For many people, there is an underlying dull fear that they might be exposed as a fraud whether at work, in marriage, in parenting, or in life in general. Have you been there? Start by admitting that you don't have it all together, that you don't have it all figured out or planned out ahead of time. Continue by telling God out loud how often you have faked it and how desperate you are for someone (hopefully Him) to help you spin all the plates you need to spin and be willing to let drop those that need to drop. Then ask Him to come and pick up all the scraps and pieces. You might have heard of *The Ed Sullivan Show* (1948–1971) where a man came on the show and spun plates on thin wooden sticks. He kept them all going but was running like crazy from one to the next. From what we saw on television, he didn't drop one plate. I drop them, it seems, every day—maybe even multiple times a day.

As long as I believe I should keep those plates of life spinning (career, marriage, parenting, success, money, meaning) by myself, I am living a lie, a falsehood. Whenever I recognize that I *cannot* and *should not* be trying to manage all those aspects (or any of them for that matter) by myself without God, I come in line with God's reality—*truth*. In those times, I am living in integrity because the core of me is designed by God to be in relationship, first with Him and second with other people. We were never meant to make it on our own. We were created in God's image (God the Father, Son, and Holy Spirit) (Genesis 1:26), and God said, "It is not good that man should be alone" (Genesis 2:18).

Faith is about believing with an attitude of humility that what God said *is*, even if we haven't experienced the fulfillment of His Word (Hebrews 11). It requires me to have integrity that although my senses may tell me one thing, the image of God Himself calls us far beyond our senses and into the depth of the reality of His love and into relationship with others. First we must receive His love.

Chapter 3

Love

*I was sitting in the mud puddle of myself
instead of playing at the ocean of your love.*

You may remember me saying at some point in our times together, "I believe the Bible follows the rules of mathematics and story problems." When you say the word *is* in story problems, you may recall that it is the equivalent of "equals." So when the Bible says "God is love" (1 John 4:16), it is saying that God equals love, and conversely, love equals God.[2]

When you see and experience true love consistent with the character of God, you are experiencing God's presence in a tangible way. The only way we can truly understand this in an increasing and growing capacity is to receive the intimacy and love of God. This, I believe, begins with humility. I must intentionally move away from the pride that looks like this in me: "I've got this. I can do it myself. I don't need anyone to tell me, help me, correct me, guide me, or support me. I will figure it out and muscle through it until I succeed." I see God responding to that attitude over and over again with something that looks like this: "Okay, I'll let you try, but you won't get there on your own. Because I am gentle and patient, I will let you, but I am right here when you realize you need me."

I am convinced that the way to understand God's love more fully and completely is to go through (by the way of) humility. We cannot understand God's love without being willing to receive His love. That means we receive Him and all of who He is. I made the statement in Chapter 2 that "the only place faith can grow is in the soil of humility."

---

[2] I understand there will be some who would like to debate this on a philosophical or theological basis. What I am saying is that true love, defined by God's character, does not exist apart from God and His presence. God does not exist apart from the love that is fundamentally Him.

I believe this is also true of God-like, or true, love. The only place true love can grow is in the soil of humility.

We usually view humility as the opposite of pride. If that is the case, I see pride as a focus on self and self interest and humility as a focus on and concern for others. We can see this in the intimate relationship of God the Father, God the Son, and God the Holy Spirit. Philippians 2:1–11 clearly lays out this humility between God the Father and God the Son.

> So if there is any encouragement in Christ, any comfort from love, any participation in the Spirit, any affection and sympathy, complete my joy by being of the same mind, having the same love, being in full accord and of one mind. Do nothing from selfish ambition or conceit, but in humility count others more significant than yourselves. Let each of you look not only to his own interests, but also to the interests of others. Have this mind among yourselves, which is yours in Christ Jesus, who, though he was in the form of God, did not count equality with God a thing to be grasped, but emptied himself, by taking the form of a servant, being born in the likeness of men. And being found in human form, he humbled himself by becoming obedient to the point of death, even death on a cross. Therefore God has highly exalted him and bestowed on him the name that is above every name, so that at the name of Jesus every knee should bow, in heaven and on earth and under the earth, and every tongue confess that Jesus Christ is Lord, to the glory of God the Father.

Humility is also central in the relationship between God the Father, God the Son, and God the Holy Spirit.

> Jesus said to him, "Have I been with you so long, and you still do not know me, Philip? Whoever has seen me

has seen the Father. How can you say, 'Show us the Father'? Do you not believe that I am in the Father and the Father is in me? The words that I say to you I do not speak on my own authority, but the Father who dwells in me does his works. Believe me that I am in the Father and the Father is in me, or else believe on account of the works themselves. Truly, truly, I say to you, whoever believes in me will also do the works that I do; and greater works than these will he do, because I am going to the Father. Whatever you ask in my name, this I will do, that the Father may be glorified in the Son. If you ask me anything in my name, I will do it. If you love me, you will keep my commandments. And I will ask the Father, and he will give you another Helper, to be with you forever, even the Spirit of truth, whom the world cannot receive, because it neither sees him nor knows him. You know him, for he dwells with you and will be in you. I will not leave you as orphans; I will come to you. Yet a little while and the world will see me no more, but you will see me. Because I live, you also will live. In that day you will know that I am in my Father, and you in me, and I in you. Whoever has my commandments and keeps them, he it is who loves me. And he who loves me will be loved by my Father, and I will love him and manifest myself to him." Judas (not Iscariot) said to him, "Lord, how is it that you will manifest yourself to us, and not to the world?" Jesus answered him, "If anyone loves me, he will keep my word, and my Father will love him, and we will come to him and make our home with him. Whoever does not love me does not keep my words. And the word that you hear is not mine but the Father's who sent me. These things I have spoken to you while I am still with you. But the Helper, the Holy Spirit, whom the Father will send in my name, he will teach you all things and bring to your remembrance all that I have said to you. Peace I leave with you; my peace I give to you. Not as the world gives do I give to you. Let not your hearts be troubled, neither let them be afraid. You heard me say to you, 'I am going away, and I will come to you.' If you loved me, you would have rejoiced, because I am going to the Father, for the Father is greater than I. And now I have told you before it takes place, so that when it does take place you may believe. I will no longer talk much with you, for the ruler of this world is coming. He has no claim on me, but I do as the Father has commanded me, so that the world may know that I love the Father. Rise, let us go from here." (John 14:9–31)

But when the Helper comes, whom I will send to you from the Father, the Spirit of truth, who proceeds from the Father, he will bear witness about me. And you also will bear witness, because you have been with me from the beginning. (John 15:26–27)

I have said all these things to you to keep you from falling away. They will put you out of the synagogues. Indeed, the hour is coming when whoever kills you will think he is offering service to God. And they will do these things because they have not known the Father, nor me. But I have said these things to you, that when their hour comes you may remember that I told them to you. I did not say these things to you from the beginning, because I was with you. But now I am going to him who sent me, and none of you asks me, "Where are you going?" But because I have said these things to you, sorrow has filled your heart. Nevertheless, I tell you the truth: it is to your advantage that I go away, for if I do not go away, the Helper will not come to you. But if I go, I will send him to you. And when he comes, he will convict the world concerning sin and righteousness and judgment: concerning sin, because they do not believe in me; concerning righteousness, because I go to the Father, and you will see me no longer; concerning judgment, because the ruler of this world is judged. I still have many things to say to you, but you cannot bear them now. When the Spirit of truth comes, he will guide you into all the truth, for he will not speak on his own authority, but whatever he hears he will speak, and he will declare to you the things that are to come. He will glorify me, for he will take what is mine and declare it to you. All that the Father has is mine; therefore I said that he will take what is mine and declare it to you. (John 16:1–15)

I see in these passages that "giving to and receiving from each other" is their humility instead of "taking from or forcing on," which is characteristic of pride. I hope you can see this in the relationships among God the Father, the Son, and the Holy Spirit. This is the intimate love in humility—otherness that the Triune God welcomes us into, not only with Himself but also with each other.

You have seen pride in me many times as I have focused on myself and my self-interest. I pray that you have also seen over time that I have slowly moved away from a focus on myself to a genuine compassion in action toward others. All of this had to be in the strength of knowing and believing who God made me to be. I know it wasn't by myself. I hope you have experienced times when I have not been so concerned about my way, my agenda, my timing, and my comfort as I am about the needs, the pain, the trouble, the grief, the happiness, the growth, the accomplishments, or the efforts of others around me. Even as I write this my heart grieves over the times I know I did *not* live that out. Once again, please forgive me. At the same time, I hope you have been able to give your love to me and that I have been willing and open to receive from you without blocking you and your love toward me.

This is where intimacy in love is important. When I asked what intimacy is, one of my students in Uganda said, "In-to-me-see." I had never heard intimacy defined that way. It is so true and very memorable. In intimacy, I let you see into me, and you let me see into you. What does that mean? One of the ways to understand it is found in the Psalms. Look at how the psalmists (writers of the psalms) express their hearts to God. Here is a generalized sampling of their intimacy.

> Psalm 30 – gratefulness
> Psalm 31 – pleading
> Psalm 33 – praise
> Psalm 35 – appeal
> Psalm 42 – passion and pain
> Psalm 48 – awe
> Psalm 51 – guilt and repentance
> Psalm 54 – fear
> Psalm 55 – betrayal

This is mankind expressing intimacy and openness toward God. In the Psalms, we can also see God expressing openness and desire for intimacy. In Psalm 50, He reveals Himself as judge, but in many other places in the Bible, He opens Himself up to us, His created beings.

> Job 38–41 – here is who I AM
> Isaiah 40 – compassion
> Isaiah 50, 55 – offer of relationship
> Isaiah 58 – appeal to come to Him
> Malachi 1 – love and pain
> Malachi 3 – pain of betrayal

Intimacy in love calls those in the relationship into a willingness to express the full extent of their desire, hope, pain, and sorrow. When I close off and guard my heart, intimacy is hindered even if I guard only a fraction of who I am. That fraction of me will never experience intimacy until it is exposed. No matter how much I desire complete intimacy, guarding that fraction will keep me from giving and receiving wholehearted love. What if I gave you this book, but as I hand it to you I rip out some of the pages and hold them back? What would you feel? So often we want an open-hearted intimacy in love with God and with others, but we are too fearful because somewhere along the way we have gotten hurt one too many times by someone—someone close, which is especially painful. So I decide in my heart that I will open it this far and no farther. I wonder why no one gets close to me and why no one loves me when, in fact, I am keeping my heart from being loved.

A woman who came to see me gave me permission to tell her story. When she came to me on a summer Kansas morning, she was covered with a winter parka and hood. She sat down and pulled her knees up onto the chair. We worked through many things in her life, especially bitterness toward her father. Over time, protecting herself was no longer an issue, and she was able to love and be loved. God, in His grace, released her to love.

I am in the process of learning this. Just in the last month, I realized I was guarding my heart from those I "feel" are trying to take love from me. God revealed that I would pull away from those people out of fear that I might somehow be drained of "me." I'm not sure what I thought would happen in the end, but that perception, right or wrong, kept me from intimacy. What if I were willing to completely, intimately, and openly receive God's love and give Him my love in return? Would I be more able to open my whole heart to those God directed me to—in His way and in His time? "We love because he first loved us" (1 John 4:19).

If I am willing to believe, I will find out that He is worthy for me to receive His love. Therefore, I could increasingly love others. I won't have to guard my heart because I believe He loves me so much that He guards my heart. He doesn't guard it from getting hurt. As Philippians 4:7 says, it is the peace of God that guards your heart. So what is the peace of God guarding me from? It guards me from fear, anxiety, worry, and the what-ifs of life that eat us from the inside out. Behind these what-ifs that we try to control slithers the same question from the Garden of Eden: "Did God really say?" Did He really say He loves me? Could He really love me?

Here is where I want to pause and ask you, my child, this: What do you believe about Jesus? There is always a cost to genuinely answer this question—*always*. Oh, you can half-heartedly answer this question or not bother answering it at all. But I believe there is a cost. "Whoever believes in him is not condemned, but whoever does not believe is condemned already, because he has not believed in the name of the only Son of God" (John 3:18). Saying no or ignoring the question (which is also saying no) is unbelief, which is already being condemned—the cost is eternal. However, if you are willing to explore that possibility that Jesus could or did do something that looks like love, He was talking to you when He was quoting a prophecy about Himself. "Behold, my servant whom I have chosen, my beloved with whom my soul is well pleased. I will put my Spirit upon him, and he will proclaim justice to the Gentiles. He will not quarrel or cry aloud, nor will anyone hear his voice in the streets; a bruised reed he will not break, and a smoldering wick he will not quench, until he brings justice to victory; and in his name the Gentiles will hope" (Matthew 12:18–21).

Understand that if you choose to explore this, there is also a cost. Are you willing to risk all you think you know, are, and have in this truly temporary life to gain eternity with God and gain more than you could ever think or imagine? Being willing to, by faith, believe what Jesus has done and will do in you is described in more detail in the Appendix at the end of this book. So if this is you right now, go check it out. This book will begin to make a lot more sense when you open your heart and decide to let Jesus's love enter. Go ahead. After you do that, come back here or even start at the beginning of the book again.

There are costs to loving God. I need you to know the costs your mom and I have paid in life to love God with increasingly open hearts. One of those costs is to believe. I asked you to decide if you have paid the cost to believe. You can't be half in. I tried for most of my early life to be half in. It tore me apart. I had to fake it. I was constantly aware of how I was appearing and what I was saying, in *fear* that I would be exposed.

When I chose to get serious with my faith—truly serious—I was starting as an associate pastor. I realized before arriving in Clay Center, Kansas, that I could not truly lead these people to God if I were not going to God myself. At least I could not do it with integrity. I have always loved getting up early. The decision to go to the church very early in the morning was a joy for me given by God. (Find your own way that God has already put in you, and don't quit.) My choice to get increasingly real and raw with God came with a price. First, I didn't know how to do that since I had lived a double life (the outside persona then the inside self-centered persona). I had to humble myself and ask God to help me. I didn't know what I didn't know about myself. That was the cry of my heart. I kept coming back to this: "Expose who I really am. And if I'm not getting it, speak more clearly and more loudly." That is when some of the early cases started to reveal themselves.

One of those cases was a person who walked into my office and said, "Tim, do you know what your problem is? You have a lot of pride." Of course, my first thought was, "You're one to talk!" Later, when I asked God about it, the Holy Spirit reminded me of my prayer that He would speak more clearly and more loudly. That was pretty clear, God. And this person was correct. After continuing that cry for God to expose my heart so I could repent, I was in a church leadership meeting. I was a young associate pastor. The oldest person in the room, after reading some Scripture about rebellious leaders, said, "All of us around this table are rebellious." Then that same person leaned over, looked at me, and said, "But Tim, you're the most rebellious one here." My fleshly reaction was to get up and hit the guy. My second reaction was to make his argument invalid by invalidating him (in my mind). *He has never come to me one-on-one*, I thought. *How unbiblical! That's not how believers are supposed to act.*

By the time the meeting was over, of which I remember nothing else, I was a smoldering heap of fury. At the end of the closing prayer, I quickly left the room and went to my office. I got out some paper and something to write with and erupted, "Okay, God!" I prayed. "Show me if, indeed, I am rebellious." Eight or nine situations flowed onto the paper. I couldn't write fast enough. Then it was over. "Why that way, God? That was so wrong of him." The Holy Spirit deep in me prompted my heart that I wasn't hearing any other way. These were very small costs of beginning to give up my "holy" view of "holy me" that deep down I knew wasn't true.

In the midst of all this, I was still consistently setting aside time with God to be as real as I believed I could be. Sometimes I yelled at God because I accused Him of not caring for the congregation. I would look over the empty pews and in my mind review the pain and suffering of various people who sat there. God would gently show me the people. He also showed me in that view of the congregation the church staff who were caring for them. At another point, I was calling the Bride of Christ, His Church, all kinds of names, including nasty, backbiting, and hypocritical. Somewhere in the middle of all those names I realized I had to include myself in the Bride. Finally, my rant ran out. I believe the Holy Spirit asked if I was done. That started a few more names I thought of. Again, "Are you done now?" Nothing else came readily to mind, so I conceded the floor to the God of the universe. (How gracious of me, huh?) What He said to me next took me literally to my knees in tears. "I know," God said. "But I love the Bride, and she is beautiful." I knew in the depth of my soul I was included in that beautiful rabble. Even now tears come to my eyes, and they come every time I tell this story.

This "cost"—opening myself up or letting God open me up and reveal the ugliness inside—was whittling away my facade. It was brutally honest from my point of view, but it was also graciously truthful from God to me—often painfully so. A sharp turning point came. I had this sense that I was pursuing God, but there seemed to be an invisible barrier. I would grow and then not be able to get past a certain depth (or height) of relationship with God, like I was bouncing off the ceiling. I started to plead with God to reveal what was standing in the way.

Regularly, I came back to my desire for some deeper relationship with God but had to leave it in His hands. Then one day as I was driving and praising God for His goodness, a still, small, gentle voice—a heart-prompting of the Holy Spirit—said, "Tell your wife about your sexual sin."[3] God had already graciously freed me from a couple of these areas, so I responded, "But that would ruin our marriage." His answer? "Okay." "What do you mean, okay? You just told me to tell Kim, and I said no. How can that be okay?" "Okay. Our relationship will not grow anymore. It will stay the same." I knew I couldn't do that. At that point, I completely let go and said in tears, "I trust You. I don't believe You put this marriage together just to watch it fall apart because I obey You. I will obey. I know You will somehow take care of Kim. You will take

---

[3] I am intentionally leaving out the details because so many of you are in your own struggle with this, and I want you to know that I'm no different. I've been there, and except by God's grace I would still be there. Maybe the details are different, but I am also on my journey.

care of our two little kids, whether I see them often or not at all. I know You will take care of me no matter what I do or where I go. I trust You, and I will obey."

The few days after I told Kim were earth-shattering for her. A few days later, she came to me and said, "There is nothing you can do to pay for what you did to me. I'm going to have to pay. But ultimately it is Jesus who has to pay for what you did." We decided to watch some counseling videos that a group was going through. We had missed the first one, so we watched it at home that night. Some of the first words out of the counselor's mouth were, "There is nothing a person who has sinned against you can pay for the pain they have caused you. You have to choose to pay for that pain." This was the beginning of our healing journey.

Unfortunately, although this was the beginning of healing, my lies, deception, and dual life lessened but continued. God kept calling me into integrity and truth deeper and deeper in every area of my life. He also called me deeper into love expressed toward Him in obedience.

One of the first acts of obedience was to give up my plans for our tenth anniversary Caribbean vacation in order to go for a week of training to counsel others in the same way we were helped. As God called us to help others through their pain and sin, we were seeing God transform lives and do miracles. Within two years, some leaders in the church decided I wasn't doing what I was called to do and suggested I be released to do what God was doing through me. The decision-making leadership unanimously (by a movement of the Holy Spirit visibly changing hearts) voted to release me. We were shocked and confused, but God showed us clearly that His hand was in it and it was time for us to go.

The next major step of obedience that I believe cost us dearly was encouraging integrity in a counseling ministry I was leading in part—the very counseling ministry that had trained us. Around six months later, the founder resigned and took many donors with him. That led to a financial decline in the donation-based ministry. Not long after that, we were released because of lack of funds in the ministry.

We believed God was calling us to work in a children's center on Uganda, so we sold or gave away much of what we had to move our family to Uganda. The cost was bigger since it also deeply affected our children, Kara and Micah, in many ways. Together as a family, we saw God tangibly and clearly leading us. It was there that I thrived the most since it seemed like God was growing me deeper into helping and loving people. Relationships grew deep as well, especially with the family group we were a part of. We grew to love these children deeply, and eventually we were asked to take four of the older boys into our home—four who were beginning to transition into adulthood.

When we were asked to come to Uganda, I was originally asked to help the leadership understand why they were losing the hearts of the older children. I was to find out why many were turning their hearts away from God. After five years of consistently bringing these areas to my immediate supervisor, Kim and I realized we needed to write a five-year report outlining some of these key areas that we believed were causing these effects. The process of writing, presenting the report, and having conversation about the report was all done in obedience surrounded by a lot of prayer. Yet we were told to resign, and other difficulties and pain followed.

All this happened while we were back in the United States on home assignment. Our belongings were back in Uganda. We had planned a year of meeting family and supporters, which we continued although now with a very different focus—prayer for what God had next for us, thanksgiving for each supporter, and glory to God for sustaining us through it all.

The unexpected termination forced us to rather quickly plan a trip to Uganda to pack our belongings and say goodbye. While we did this at the children's center, we were under strict supervision. All of this caused huge costs relationally, emotionally, physically, spiritually, and financially, not only in those days but some even today. This love we have for God costs us significantly when out of love for Jesus we obey. It changes not only us but those we are connected to, even remotely.

How did your mom and I get to this place of loving God so much that we were willing to risk almost everything? We were one step closer to the heart of Jesus in little steps of faith-generated obedience.

Chapter 4

Obedience

When my food is to do God's will,
suffering because of obedience brings joy.

For me, risking everything because of love for God started from a place of not being eager to risk much of anything for anyone. As you read in the previous chapter, I was only half-in as a Christ-follower early on in my life. Oh, I deceived myself and believed I was completely all in when I knew in my heart that wasn't true. James 1:8 talks about a double-minded man unstable in all his ways. That was me, living on the outside like I was a good Christian pastor's kid. Meanwhile, on the inside I wanted to do what I wanted to do. I had to come up with many ways to keep up my appearance. I was always keeping track of what story I told to whom. In the midst of the lies that I told myself and others, the deception eventually betrayed me and consumed me. That sounds very similar to the One Ring in Tolkien's *Lord of the Rings*. My hypocrisy encased me from relationships in arrogance and self-absorption. By and through the grace of God, I began to honestly and deeply call out to Him to rescue me from *me*.

Because of all my self-deception and self-absorption, my college years were confusing. I longed to have a relationship with God that others talked about, so I put myself in places where those types of people passed through. I tried to pursue people who were, I believed, authentic and genuine. I wanted to be near them, but at the same time, I was keenly aware of how my character was diametrically opposed to theirs (at least I thought so). I often heard of these types of people listening to God. I knew many of the people of the Bible talked to God and listened to Him. Even my parents and many in the church where I grew up said they listened to God.

By the end of my second to the last year at the university, I was getting desperate to figure out what I was going to do with my life. Since I had heard so much about listening to God, I decided to get very serious about this listening thing. I was pretty much clueless about how to do it, but I decided to take a blank piece of paper, (Yes, I took only one piece of paper. I didn't think God was saying too much to me anyway and that one should suffice.) I used a pencil in case I had to change something. I got on my bike, rode to the nearest park, found an empty table, and sat down with my pencil and paper in front of me. I said to God, maybe out loud, "I'm going to sit right here and try to hear from You. And I'll sit here until you tell me what to do with my life." I pictured myself sitting all through the afternoon until it got dark and then sitting there all through the night and, who knows, maybe all the next day. I was determined—and desperate.

I remember many thoughts coming into my head about things I had to get done, people I needed to talk to, and memories. For each one that came up, I mentally and gently pushed them aside and tried to make my mind blank. (I don't necessarily recommend this method.)

Less than a half hour went by when a thought came to my mind. "Continue your plan to go to seminary to become a pastor."[4] In a split second I recognized that I had this as an option, but it was clearer than I had ever encountered. This did not seem like the muddled thoughts I had in the past. In fact, it seemed crystal clear and resonated with my whole being. But then it (I believe "it" was God) said in the shape of a thought, "Keep your mind open to being a missionary to Koreans." Now that rocked me. I knew of Koreans but didn't feel I knew any personally. I certainly never had even an inkling of a thought that I would be a missionary. This was my lesson in listening—my first lesson. I kept asking, "Is there more?" Silence. After about another half hour, I gave up. I came, I asked, and I received. I got back on my bike and started riding out of the park when I noticed lots of dark-haired people praying around some picnic tables under a shelter. As I followed the path around

---

[4] You might remember that I was fourth in a line of pastors and was often asked if would be a pastor like my father, grandfather, and great-grandfather. I enjoyed counseling and helping people, but not preaching until I was about halfway through my university years. Then it became a vague idea I had in my head, from my own making, I thought.

the shelter, I looked up and almost fell off my bike. There was a sign hanging from the roof of the shelter that read, "Korean Friends Church." It was all I could do to hold back my elation through laughter until I reached the parking lot. God had spoken to me! From then on I was very open to listening, although not always very attentive and very poor at responding to God speaking.

A number of encounters in seminary with professors, spiritual directors, seminars, and classes opened my eyes and ears to the joy of the mystery of listening in prayer (communion and communing with God). It wasn't until I began practicing it almost every day that I started to discern the Holy Spirit prompting me in my spirit (in other words, talking to me). It sounds crazy, but it was as simple as pausing and asking God, "Where in Scripture do You want me to go as I read today?" When nothing would come to mind, I continued with the devotional I was currently reading.

One day, early in the morning and early on in practicing listening and trying to respond in obedience, a certain psalm came to mind, and I read it. Bear in mind that this was a time in my life when I thought all was well. The psalm, on the other hand, seemed to be about difficulty and hardship. I was surprised and concerned at the same time. I asked God if this was about impending doom in the future of my life, or was it for someone else. Or possibly was this the true cry of my heart, and I just didn't realize it? I asked, and I waited—and waited. No response (that I recognized). Eventually, I ran out of time that morning. I said to God, "I'm not sure why You gave me this today. It seems out of place, but I expect You will show me.

I went about my day's plans. About mid-morning, I received a phone call from a woman in the church I was pastoring. She asked me to visit her father in the hospital. I knew her, but I did not know him. When I visited him, he and I had a little conversation, but his daughter talked more. When it was time for me to leave, she asked me to read something from the Bible, maybe a psalm. Immediately this psalm I had read earlier came to mind, so I read it. Part of the way through, I noticed that the woman was crying. I asked her if she wanted me to stop, but she said, "No, please finish it." When I finished, she thanked me and asked why I had chosen that psalm. I told her that as I was attempting to listen to God earlier in that morning, the psalm had come to my mind, but I didn't know why. She said with tears streaming down her face, "This was the psalm that was read at my mother's funeral, and as a family, we have read it every time we get together." Coincidence? I believe it was the prompting voice of the Holy Spirit revealing the heart of the Father—compassion for His children. He drew me in to be a vessel and a servant of His heart.

When I talk to people about listening to God, the most common question I am asked is this: "How do you know it is God?" I believe we have only two choices: God or Satan. As many say, "What if it is just my own thoughts?" We are either agreeing with God and bringing about good in the world consistent with His character, or we are agreeing with Satan and bringing about selfishness and destruction. Is it our own thought to bring about good? The first chapter of James has a lot to say about that. Actually the whole book of James addresses this directly or indirectly. "Every good gift and every perfect gift is from above, coming down from the Father of lights, with whom there is no variation or shadow due to change" (James 1:17).

If it is producing good fruit, it must come from God, but the only way to determine it is to intentionally submit it to God's judgment. "God, is this right? Is this from You?" That question can only be answered or judged in relationship with God. James writes about asking for wisdom and includes "in faith" and "not doubting." I read that and realized I need to expect that God is talking to me and then act on what He says. Afterward, regardless of the circumstances that come out of that obedience, I have to ask, "Did I hear You right?" I am asking Him in relationship and communicating with Him. I am not trying to decide if I made the right decision based on the results of what I experienced. Otherwise, I am deciding whether I heard God right rather than letting Him tell me whether I heard Him right.

You might ask, "What if I still don't know?" Believe. I believe that is exactly what James is talking about. Try it out, but stay in that constant communication with God and in that consistent relationship with those whose hearts reflect Him. If not, we miss opportunity after opportunity of obedience because we fear our own lack rather than boldly stepping out in faith. This is the way we grow in faith and wisdom.

When we go to God to let Him judge, He will correct us if necessary. He will give wisdom generously without finding fault. But if we doubt, we stay within our own thoughts, our own weaknesses, our own failures, our own mistakes, and our own fears. We don't risk and grow by default into a dynamic relationship with God who has all wisdom.

If you're wondering how to get started, first set aside time to practice, listening in silence without distractions (by choice—without music playing, TV on, phone notifications continuously beeping, or maybe not even having your phone near you if it is too distracting). Ask a question, and be aware of inner responses. If they are thoughts that tear you down or tell you that you aren't worth an answer or that God is angry with you and doesn't want to talk to you, those are lies from the enemy. Does our sin hinder our ability to hear? Absolutely. If a specific current sin comes to mind, that is God talking. He wants to address it in you. If a vague feeling about being unworthy or a general category of sin comes to mind, ask God to address the sin specifically. Talk with Him about that sin. Be honest with God. Ask for His wisdom. If a specific course of action comes to mind, ask Him how He wants you to carry it out. If it has to do with cheating, lying, deception, twisting the truth, or other ways that are characteristic of the enemy's ways, question that course of action, and ask God to reveal the motives you might have.

Understand that deliberate and willful disobedience will complicate, cloud, and color our discernment of whether God is speaking or the enemy is disguising his voice as ours. Our own selfish desires are the issue. "But each person is tempted when he is lured and enticed by his own desire" (James 1:14). We can ask God what He thinks about our sin. Again, this takes time, effort, practice, and patience. It also depends on God as we are brutally honest internally before Him. What am I avoiding? What do I think is impossible in God's interaction with me?

We can ask God to make us aware of Him all day long in the little things we notice or that come to mind. I think the following is a very practical application. "We destroy arguments and every lofty opinion raised against the knowledge of God, and take every thought captive to obey Christ" (2 Corinthians 10:5). Not long after asking God to reveal Himself throughout my day, a small, blue butterfly caught my eye as I was walking. The bright baby blue creature stunned me enough to notice it, and then it disappeared when it landed with its wings together. It was the same color as the ground, but as I got closer, it flew away again, showing that stunning blue. Immediately, my request to God came to mind. He was revealing His presence through the beauty and mystery of that little butterfly. I thanked Him for being there and for revealing His presence. Not long after that, I told someone about it, and almost immediately I saw the same type of butterfly in a totally different location. "Thank You, Father, for a little bit of Your glory revealed in a butterfly. You are confirming Your presence through Your creation every moment of every day if I will only notice."

The little things matter. When the Holy Spirit prompts me to respond in obedience to His command, His gentleness looks like an option. It's not. Oh, you can choose. We have been given that choice to follow our selfish desires that are on the throne of our hearts (Satan's plan for us). We also have been given an opportunity to profoundly receive the grace and the glory of God in faith. This is God's transforming work in us that we cannot boast in other than in our weakness that requires His rescue.

My friend John, a resident doctor, had been battling over and over for freedom from giving into temptation. He prayed fervently to be free. After a long battle, one day in a hospital cafeteria he accidentally dropped a knife into the trash. Immediately, there was an inner prompting (he and I would both say the Holy Spirit was speaking to him) to pick up the knife. The arguments ran through his head: *I'm not going to pick it up. It's probably worth five cents. Besides, I'm a resident doctor. What would people think if I were digging in the trash? The cafeteria is full of people. No! I will not pick up the knife.* He walked out of the cafeteria, all the while hearing, "Pick up the knife." Down the hall, he heard, "Pick up the knife." The elevator doors opened. "Pick up the knife." "No!" On the elevator, "Pick up the knife." Up three floors, "Pick up the knife." Off the elevator, "Pick up the knife." Elevator doors close. "Pick up the knife." "Okay! I'll pick up the knife." Down three floors, back into the cafeteria, there on top of the trash in a virtually empty cafeteria was the knife. He picked it up and put it on the conveyor belt to be washed. He said that within twenty-four hours, his desire to give in to that specific type of sin was gone. The only thing he could think was that he was obedient in the little stuff, and God was honoring his obedience and setting him free from the big stuff.

I don't believe obeying in small things always directly leads to freedom from big sins. I do believe, however, that every step of obedience, no matter how difficult, simple, or seemingly insignificant is honored by God as extremely important and glorifying to Him. I also believe that when we obey in ways that are simple or seem insignificant to us, it makes our hearts more responsive to obey. We can hear His voice more clearly. Then our heart's desires begin to change.

You know that your mom used to ride her horse in shows. A well-trained horse is attentive and responsive to very subtle cues from the rider. I experienced this when I rode Iceland horses with her in Sweden. A slight nudge of my knee, and my horse would respond. I want to respond to God that way. I am trying to respond to the most quiet voice and nudge, and trying to remember to check in with Him. "Did I hear You correctly?" Oh, but my stubbornness and my I-have-a-better-idea rebellion rears its head quite often. "Lord, help me out of my unbelief." Three verses stand out for me.

> Blessed is the man who walks not in the counsel of the wicked, nor stands in the way of sinners, nor sits in the seat of scoffers; but his delight is in the law of the LORD, and on his law he meditates day and night. He is like a tree planted by streams of water that yields its fruit in its season, and its leaf does not wither. In all that he does, he prospers. (Psalm 1:1–3)

What company do I keep? Are they people who mock everyone and everything? Or do I keep company with God's Word and those who honor God's Word, not just in theological debates but in day-to-day living it out? "Finally, brothers, whatever is true, whatever is honorable, whatever is just, whatever is pure, whatever is lovely, whatever is commendable, if there is any excellence, if there is anything worthy of praise, think about these things" (Philippians 4:8).

Where do my thoughts go, and do I let them run away with me or capture them, submit them to the throne of God, and turn my heart to those things listed in Philippians 4:8? What if I made a list of things that are true, things that are honorable, things that are just, pure, lovely, commendable, excellent, or worthy of praise. I have never done this, but even as I write about capturing my thoughts, this idea came to mind. What do you think about? Would this or could this be a great way to turn our random thoughts into obedient thoughts? This is a perfect example of what I have tried to live. In fact, I'm going to stop writing and do it now.[5]

I started the list, and I know it will be helpful. But it wasn't as easy as I thought. In fact, it will have to be ongoing because some words I found very difficult and listed only a couple of items under them. Thinking on things listed in Philippians 4:8 can seem like an insignificant area of obedience until we start living it—I mean *truly* living it and seeing God transform our lives in response to our obedience. This is exactly where this book is intended to lead you (or I should say "us")—into loving God by our obedience. I've been reading James, and this is, I believe, one of James's main points: faith lived out in obedience is considered by God as righteousness. If we follow the flow of Scripture, we'll see that Jesus says the most important two commands are to love God with all we are and to love our neighbor as ourselves. But then Jesus, on the night he was betrayed, gave us a new command that didn't abolish the old commands. He gave us a command that more clearly and precisely portrayed His heart behind the commands. He said, "This is my commandment, that you love one another as I have loved you" (John 15:12). What does that mean? It starts back in John 15:9: "As the Father has loved me, so have I loved you. Abide in my love." Jesus is saying, "I love you as the Father has loved me." How? "Because I remain in the Father's love."

---

[5] Update: I did make lists of everything I thought represented those words. It was harder than I thought. I spent a few days concentrating on them and then forgot I had written them. I have come back to them periodically, but this is reminding me to deliberately focus on them.

What was the evidence that He was remaining in God's love? He explained that in the next verse, and it had everything to do with obedience. "If you keep my commandments, you will abide in my love, just as I have kept my Father's commandments and abide in his love" (John 15:10). How did Jesus live this out? It was His sustenance. You might remember that He told his disciples, "I have food to eat that you do not know about" (John 4:32). Then He explained what He meant: "My food is to do the will of him who sent me and to accomplish his work" (John 4:34). This is what fed Jesus when he experienced physical hunger as Satan tempted him to do His own thing rather than obey His Father. Jesus chose His Father's will to be fulfilled completely, not just temporarily, filled.

Let's go back to John 15:12, "This is my commandment, that you love one another as I have loved you," and the question, "What does it mean to love each other as Jesus loves me?" He loved us by obeying the Father fully and laying down his life for his friends. Once again, he explained himself. "You are my friends if you do what I command you" (John 15:14). This has to rest on the previous verse: "Greater love has no one than this, that someone lay down his life for his friends" (John 15:13).

I once said to your mom, "I would die for you." She responded, "I don't want you to die for me. I want you to live for me day after day." Jesus was saying that ultimately when it comes down to it, will you be willing to love so much day after day that you would be willing to die for someone. He hadn't yet died, but He was saying that He lives on following His Father's commands. He knows His Father will take care of His needs, so all He has to do is obey. His obedience is an expression of His love, and it is the very thing that fulfills Him.

It seems to me that Jesus's expression of love toward His Father required Him to be in constant communion (which includes communication) with His Father so He would know what obedience looked like in any situation. If he learned obedience through what he suffered (Hebrews 5:8), why do we think we would have it any other way? How did He get to that place? Hebrews 5:7 tells us, "In the days of his flesh, Jesus offered up prayers and supplications, with loud cries and tears, to him who was able to save him from death, and he was heard because of his reverence." He poured out His heart to His Father, His source, His life.

We are trained or disciplined when we face hardship or opposition and then endure, depending on and submitting ourselves to Jesus, the author and perfecter of our faith (Hebrews 12:2). So our practice becomes constant (increasingly so) prayer. Remember that prayer is communion and communication with God. Our practice also includes obedience to what He guides us into, increasingly more consistent.

Do you see that both prayer and obedience are "increasingly so"? It is progression, a journey closer and closer to Jesus. We have to allow God to train us through His Word. He will do that as we take time to read, study His Word, memorize His Word, obey His Word, and listen for Him to precisely speak His Word to us through His Holy Spirit. God will also train us through experiences if we are willing to go to Him for understanding. We don't suddenly arrive. In general (not necessarily every day—there are good days and bad days), my prayers both in quantity and quality increase over months and years. My obedience increases in small ways and big ways, in obvious ways and hidden ways, and in responsiveness and consistency.

Early in my life, listening to God was once in a while. My quiet times with God, though relatively consistent, were surface and remained so because I chose to most often do what I wanted. I would obey the easy things as long as they weren't uncomfortable. I also made sure to hide and excuse my favorite sins. It wasn't until I asked God, pled with God, and cried out to God to save me from the trap I was in and enjoyed that I began to see movement. The shift came when I began to open my heart to Him.

It was around that time that I realized I needed a deep friendship with another brother (Christ-follower), someone I could be totally open with and someone who would speak truth to me face to face. I tried some mentors that I really respected, but when I got close enough, I was very disappointed. A few years went by while I prayed for and searched for someone like-hearted who I could lean on. As I was telling your mom about my search and discouragement that I couldn't find a mentor, she suggested someone. I was convinced that person was too busy, but I told her I would give him a try. So I asked John if I could tell him my story—blood, guts, and all (not literally). We drove out on a country road and parked next to a cornfield. I unloaded my story on him—all of it—the good, the bad, and the really ugly. I wasn't sure if he was going to tell me to get out of his truck and walk back to town. He didn't. Instead, he said, "That sounds a lot like my story. Can I tell you mine?" I was dumbfounded. That began a steady weekly meeting where we connected with each other. The gaps between connecting got farther apart when we moved to Uganda. But since we moved back, we have tried to touch base nearly weekly.

At the time we connected, God was already connecting me deeper into Him. I was realizing I couldn't just read a devotional and say a little prayer daily. I knew I needed Him to be infused into me and me into Him. I had to be willing to be uncomfortable in obedience. I had to take time to be quiet with my Bible and take time to record our conversation. Writing this conversation with God, I initially resisted but finally gave in. And even more basically, I had to cry out to Him to even remind me of His presence at least once between my quiet times. It's been twenty years since I started asking Him to meet me throughout my day, and I still miss His presence often. I am growing, and sometimes that is frustrating that I'm not moving faster. (Remember, this is my journey. You can try these things in a variety of ways and explore others.)

This same brother, John, even this morning was a huge encouragement to me as he gave me a gift left behind by a mutual friend who recently died. John also spoke God's truth into me, and I believe we both heard God a little more clearly in the middle of our conversation. We both needed that.

My time connecting with John over time became a discipline, a training. I had to submit myself to these times because I saw and heard from many how it is both about giving and receiving words of encouragement, words of gentle but firm correction, perspective, insight from God, outside discernment, clarity of thinking, mutual goals, and intercession.

I see this now as my own partial obedience to these verses: "And let us consider how to stir up one another to love and good works, not neglecting to meet together, as is the habit of some, but encouraging one another, and all the more as you see the Day drawing near" (Hebrews 10:24–25). Discipline and perseverance are essential to maintaining connections through the years, especially when one person moves to another town, a different part of the country, or even to another continent. I have failed to stay connected with many of you. This is the very area I have found most difficult as I try to listen to God's prompting and obey.

Chapter 5

Compassion

Compassion IS the heart of God.

Those of you who know me well enough know that at times I am lacking in the area of compassion. Some of you may feel I have been severely lacking in this area at times. I tend to agree with you. I do think many of you might say I have grown in this area amidst many ups and downs. This is the whole point in getting one step closer to Jesus. I may understand that compassion is my weakness (one of my greater weaknesses), but I also understand that compassion is fundamental to the character of God. So I ask myself this question: "How can I grow into the character of God?" God's answer to me is this: "Take one step closer to Jesus."

The road to the compassion of Jesus and therefore of our Father God may have a couple signposts along the way. For me, I see a progression from *sympathy* to *empathy* to *compassion*.

I see sympathy as noticing that a person is in some kind of pain or difficult situation and being sad for that person. As a young child, I don't remember a time that I felt sad for someone else's pain. Maybe I did and just don't remember. My first twinge of sympathy and maybe empathy came when I was the one causing the pain to a fellow student. He was a new boy at school when I was in sixth grade. I was trying desperately to fit in, and I didn't want to be seen as the new kid anymore. Someone took the comb out of the new boy's pocket and quickly tossed it to someone else. Before I knew it, a circle formed of comb keep-away. Someone tossed me the comb. At that moment my world froze. Even as I write this, I can see in my mind exactly where I was on the playground. The new kid came up to me. "Give me my comb," he said. I wish I could say I did the right thing. Nope. I did nothing but look at him, scared to death of making either decision. At that moment the playground teacher came up, and everyone—everyone except the new kid and I—scattered. As I sat in the principal's office being questioned about why I didn't give back the comb, I had a slight sadness that this kid was the new kid. I knew that wasn't easy since I had gone through it less than two years earlier. Why did I make it harder for him? Oh well, at least it wasn't me (my self-centered ways returned).

I was in my early teens before I started to listen to friends' hard situations and regularly feel sad for them. Apparently, they thought I was safe to talk to because I began to listen to their problems regularly, sometimes for hours. I don't remember ever feeling what they might have been going through (empathy). I just felt sad for them, at least until my mid-to-upper teens.

I noticed around that time that I began to put myself in their shoes. When they described their frustration, I felt frustration rising in me. I felt the betrayal they described. God began to whittle away my self-absorption, and I started a very, very slow ascent toward something that more closely resembled Jesus and the heart of God the Father. God put in my heart His image, and He is a God of compassion. In fact, it is part of His name:

> The LORD descended in the cloud and stood with him there, and proclaimed the name of the LORD. The LORD passed before him and proclaimed, "The LORD, the LORD, a God merciful and gracious, slow to anger, and abounding in steadfast love and faithfulness, keeping steadfast love for thousands, forgiving iniquity and transgression and sin, but who will by no means clear the guilty, visiting the iniquity of the fathers on the children and the children's children, to the third and the fourth generation." (Exodus 34:5–7).

God has certainly given us sympathy for people ("Ow! That must have hurt"). He has also given us empathy ("I'm crying for that person because I know what it is like to lose someone I love"). I believe compassion takes sympathy and empathy a step further. Here's what happened when the prodigal son returned home. "And he arose and came to his father. But while he was still a long way off, his father saw him and felt compassion, and ran and embraced him and kissed him" (Luke 15:20). After that, he did a lot more for his son who was in a very low condition. He put his care and love into action—compassion. This is the image of God He has put into you and me. True godly compassion, I believe, is always in action in some form or another. This is the very character of God who, in His compassion, takes action. Sometimes that action is silence because at times in our need we have to deal with (become honest with) ourselves. At that moment, God's love and care put into action through silence help us sort out what we are really asking for and seeking; that is, if we are willing to receive it.

His greatest act of compassion—entering into our pain and providing a way out—is Jesus's life on earth, His death on a cross with our sins on Him, and defeating death and the grave through His resurrection. He did not have the name Compassionate as a label just because it sounded good. He gave and took on our worst. "Have this mind among yourselves, which is yours in Christ Jesus, who, though he was in the form of God, did not count equality with God a thing to be grasped, but emptied himself, by taking the form of a servant, being born in the likeness of men. And being found in human form, he humbled himself by becoming obedient to the point of death, even death on a cross" (Philippians 2:5–8). The worst also included temptation. "For we do not have a high priest who is unable to sympathize with our weaknesses, but one who in every respect has been tempted as we are, yet without sin" (Hebrews 4:15). "In the days of his flesh, Jesus offered up prayers and supplications, with loud cries and tears, to him who was able to save him from death, and he was heard because of his reverence. Although he was a son, he learned obedience through what he suffered" (Hebrews 5:7–8).

In Chapter 3, I described how I revealed my sexual sin to your mom. In the time that followed, I knew she was justifiably angry. I asked God to give me His heart to love and care for her in that moment. I knew I didn't have the capacity to get out of my self-focused rut enough to see her and what she was going through. By God's grace, He let me view her heart, which was like a little girl who had been pushed off her bike by a bully. Her knee was skinned, and she was crying. At that point, I knew I needed to let go of the bully (me) and focus on the pain she was feeling. I asked her questions about the pain and what was hurting. Later, I remember her saying to me, "That was the first time in our marriage that I felt like you really cared about me."

I believe this went beyond my being sad that she was hurting (sympathy) or even feeling something similar (empathy). In this case, maybe for the first time in my life, I did something with compassion. I asked her questions to clarify what I thought so I could more fully grasp her situation and her pain. This was new to me, something I would learn (and am still learning) much more about. Some people describe wanting to be loved; others say they want to be valued. Others want to be noticed or seen. For some, it is feeling significant or special. When you are thirsty but haven't said anything about it or hinted about it and someone takes the effort to give you a cup of water, you know you have been noticed or seen. Some are constantly trying to be seen and rarely are. Take blind Bartimaeus, for instance (Mark 10:46–52). "He began to cry out. . . . And many rebuked him, telling him to be silent. But he cried out all the more. . . . And Jesus stopped and said, 'Call him.' . . . And Jesus said to him, 'What do you want me to do for you?'" Bartimaeus was rebuked, but Jesus saw him, called for him, and healed him. He wanted to be seen and to see.

On the other hand, the woman at the well most likely did not want to be seen, at least on the surface (John 4:6–30). Or it is possible she was so pushed out by society that it wasn't wise or safe for her to come in the cool of the morning or evening. "It was about the sixth hour [noon]. A woman from Samaria came to draw water. Jesus said to her, 'Give me a drink.'" Right away she responded in her shock, "How is it that you, a Jew, ask for a drink from me, a woman of Samaria? (For Jews have no dealings with Samaritans.)" Then Jesus, after engaging with her resistance for a short time, showed her that he sees her. "You are right in saying, 'I have no husband'; for you have had five husbands, and the one you now have is not your husband. What you have said is true.'" How did she respond? "So the woman left her water jar and went away into town and said to the people, 'Come see a man who told me all that I ever did.'" Jesus saw her, and she didn't want to be seen. But when He did see her, it was the best thing that had ever happened to her, so much so that she told everyone. Jesus had compassion on her and loved her with grace and truth.

Jesus noticed. He saw blind Bartimaeus, and he saw the woman at the well. I believe that was because His agenda was His Father's agenda, not a selfish agenda. He was concerned with His Father's will. "So Jesus said to them, 'When you have lifted up the Son of Man, then you will know that I am he, and that I do nothing on my own authority, but speak just as the Father taught me. And he who sent me is with me. He has not left me alone, for I always do the things that are pleasing to him" (John 8:28–29). "For I have come down from heaven, not to do my own will but the will of him who sent me." (John 6:38). "So Jesus said to them, 'Truly, truly, I say to you, the Son can do nothing of his own accord, but only what he sees the Father doing. For whatever the Father does, that the Son does likewise" (John 5:19).

Even right in the place of Jacob's well where Jesus met the woman, He told His disciples how important it was to do His Father's will. It is the very thing that sustained Him more than food. In fact, it *was* His food. "Jesus said to them, 'My food is to do the will of him who sent me and to accomplish his work'" (John 4:34).

Being in touch with His Father was *that* important and *that* essential. He noticed! God noticed! Jesus noticed people because He was responding to His Father and not focused on Himself. "I can do nothing on my own. As I hear, I judge, and my judgment is just, because I seek not my own will but the will of him who sent me" (John 5:30). "The one who speaks on his own authority seeks his own glory; but the one who seeks the glory of him who sent him is true, and in him there is no falsehood" (John 7:18). It is hard to see people in their hurt and pain with compassion if we are caught up in our self-focused interests.

Since this is the area I currently have the most difficulty with, I am actively working on it even as I write this book. I am finding there is a difference between having compassion for someone out of duty and having compassion for someone out of love because Christ is loving them through me. What I mean is that I can see someone, put myself in their place, and try to feel what they are feeling. I can even have a desire to meet them in the place they seem to have stated or have actually stated clearly.

I had been helping a man work through many issues in his life. One of those things was abandonment at an early age. One day, he called me and said, "I'm in excruciating pain."

"Okay, what happened?" I responded.

"My wife went to the supermarket, and I'm in excruciating pain."

Remembering his abandonment, I thought this might be touching on that memory, so to clarify, I asked him, "So when you are separated from your wife, you are in excruciating pain?"

"No. When my wife goes to the supermarket I am in excruciating pain."

I tried to meet him where I thought was logical. "Oh, that sounds hard." I wasn't meeting him where he was. I was meeting him where I thought he should be.

He got angry. "No! I'm in excruciating pain."

"Wow! That sounds really difficult," I said.

"No! I'm in excruciating pain."

That went on for a long time. I kept asking for his patience because I was really trying to understand, and I didn't know how to do that. Finally, he stopped and was silent so long that I thought we got cut off. Then he said, "When my wife goes to the supermarket, I feel like I'm getting the skin ripped off my body."

"Oh!! That's excruciating pain!" I exclaimed.

"Now you finally understand me," he said.

Did I understand how he came to that conclusion? Maybe. Did I think it was a logical conclusion from my viewpoint? No. But he finally felt understood because I took the time to try to understand where he was coming from. So the question remains, "Will I step out of my self-focus, have God's compassion for others, and truly do something about their situation? Or will I consider my desires and needs more than I do theirs and reluctantly and out of duty and obligation care for them? When I do that, I often if not always feel some sort of entitlement. "Someone needs to acknowledge what I have done. This person should appreciate me for this. Now I will expect that someone should do something for me." Or I might even think, "God, I hope You saw what I just did and that I will get some sort of benefit from it—money, ease, recreation, or at least public acknowledgment." Since I am also currently reading Ecclesiastes, I have to ask, "To what end?" What would be the benefit of receiving any of these "entitlements"? Is it because it makes me feel good? When my purpose for being "compassionate"[6] is done out of expectation that you must do something kind for me, it's like saying I will do something kind for you as long as you do something kind for me. That says my motivation for compassion is to get something out of the transaction, not because of true Christ-like love.

How do I love with Christ's love? I need to take up my cross and follow Him. Let me explain. Rather, let me quote Philippians 2:1–13 with a few comments in between.

> So if there is any encouragement in Christ, any comfort from love, any participation in the Spirit, any affection and sympathy [Paul starts by recognizing the Philippians' union with Christ, which should lead to encouragement, comfort, and sharing in the Spirit, as well as tenderness and compassion], complete my joy by being of the same mind, having the same love, being in full accord and of one mind. [If indeed that is the case, the next step is to love in unity.] Do nothing from selfish ambition or conceit, but in humility count others more significant than yourselves.

This is my opportunity to take up my cross and follow Jesus. This life isn't about me—not about what I can get (selfish ambition) or what I require others to give to me (conceit). Rather, I am to take up a public torture devise of the oppressor Rome and follow Jesus to the death of myself in order to glorify God by the full extent of loving others unselfishly. What is the full extent? It's going to the lowest place in order to obey my Father to the death of anything that gets in the way of love for Him. This is shown through obedience and love for others by serving them in compassion and humility as specifically desired through the Holy Spirit's guidance.

---

[6] This is in quotes because it is not actually compassion but rather a forced barter system.

Let each of you look not only to his own interests, but also to the interests of others. [This is where my focus must move from self-focus to other focus. This takes tremendous effort especially powered by God.] Have this mind among yourselves, which is yours in Christ Jesus, who, though he was in the form of God, did not count equality with God a thing to be grasped, but emptied himself, by taking the form of a servant, being born in the likeness of men. And being found in human form, he humbled himself by becoming obedient to the point of death, even death on a cross. Therefore God has highly exalted him and bestowed on him the name that is above every name, so that at the name of Jesus every knee should bow, in heaven and on earth and under the earth, and every tongue confess that Jesus Christ is Lord, to the glory of God the Father. Therefore, my beloved, as you have always obeyed, so now, not only as in my presence but much more in my absence, work out your own salvation with fear and trembling, for it is God who works in you, both to will and to work for his good pleasure."

There is a difference between compassion done out of duty and compassion that comes from Christ's life through me. The former leads farther and farther into self-focus, bitterness, and resentment, eventually leading to entitlement. The latter leads farther and farther into other-focus, joy, and fulfillment. Compassion out of duty keeps score and wonders why no one is doing as much as you are. Compassion of life gives, cares, and wonders to God what else you can do for this person. It is centered in relationship with the person. Why? It is centered in relationship because how else do I really know what they need if I don't find out what matters to them? It must be grounded in communion with the Holy Spirit who will truly show what is best in that moment for that person.

These are the places in my life and the other person's life that intersect. This is where the "Jesus" in me meets what the Holy Spirit is already doing in the other person's life. I believe this is where long-lasting change happens—called discipleship. Both people grow in their relationship with Jesus and in that relationship with Jesus become more one with the heart of God. That leads to wisdom. I was never looking to be more compassionate, although I should have been. I wasn't looking for the heart of God—love and compassion. Instead, I started with my greatest perceived need at the time—wisdom.[7]

---

[7] Even in the middle of typing this paragraph, I was trying to do what I thought God wanted me to do. Meanwhile, I was neglecting compassion and relationships. It is very interesting where this journey can take us. The point is to be responsive to what God is continually doing in and around us. The point is not to get things right and avoid mistakes. Quite the contrary, when I go to "getting things right" or "avoiding mistakes," it is about me, and once again, I have moved away from relationship and compassion to self-centeredness.

Chapter 6

Wisdom

*Wisdom grows from humility,
humility from wisdom with Jesus in the center.*

The first day on a new job is usually intimidating. Fresh out of seminary, knowing I had been called by God and now being called by the church in Clay Center, Kansas, to be their associate pastor, I asked, "Now what do I do?" At thirty years of age, how could I lead people in their 50s or 70s or 90s? Oh, I had brilliant ideas, but would anything work? What does it mean to work or have success in this position? I decided (absolutely by God's prompting and grace) that I needed to spend time in prayer and in His Word. I knew I needed to commit myself to go to the church early in the morning when no one else would be there to spend time with God alone. Most days I would call to Him out loud to help me know His heart. It wasn't long before I ended up in Ecclesiastes, realizing I could become similar in attitude to the writer of that book of the Bible. That seemed like a miserable place to be at the end of his life. He was trying to figure it all out on his own and came up very empty, it seemed. Why would I want that?

Part of a verse kept coming back to me. "But we have the mind of Christ" (1 Corinthians 2:16). Paul had been discussing the wisdom of the world being foolishness to God, and I wanted God's wisdom. I considered that secret and hidden wisdom decreed by God: "But we impart a secret and hidden wisdom of God, which God decreed before the ages for our glory" (1 Corinthians 2:7). I asked God for it. I knew from James and Jesus's own words that I would receive wisdom if I believed. I just wasn't sure how or when it would come, but I decided in faith that I would do my due diligence to pursue what He may have already given me.

I reasoned, maybe very simply but logically, that I would most likely find the mind of Christ and the wisdom of God in His Word. I trusted God that if I asked and then pursued in faith, He would honor

His Word. "If any of you lacks wisdom, let him ask God, who gives generously to all without reproach, and it will be given him. But let him ask in faith, with no doubting, for the one who doubts is like a wave of the sea that is driven and tossed by the wind" (James 1:5–6). Where else would I go to look for wisdom but the places that say "wisdom"? I thought that would be a good start on my search.

Quickly I landed on Proverbs 9:10: "The fear of the LORD is the beginning of wisdom, and the knowledge of the Holy One is insight." Great! Now I had another problem. What is the "fear of the Lord"? I don't ever remember a sermon, teaching, or book that taught me what the fear of the Lord really means. That question launched me on a journey to seek God, and that journey hasn't ended after twenty-five years. It began with a need to have wisdom, and I cried out to God who promptly showed me my need to understand and live in the fear of Him.

How do we learn about the fear of God? The easy American way would be to search for books. So that's what I did, and I found very few. What was option two? Search Scripture. I believe I started with a concordance, a good place to start a word study in the Bible. That took me back to the verse that started it, Proverbs 9:10. I remembered other word studies I had done using cross references, so I started cross-referencing the "fear of God." It opened my study exponentially. One verse referenced two or three more verses. Each of those expanded to two, even four more. So before I knew it, I had pages of verses. Then the Holy Spirit reminded me of other verses I had read throughout the years. I found them and connected them. I finally had to start categorizing all these verses so I could keep track of them. The Holy Spirit connected my study with devotionals, articles, other studies, and a few books I happened to find. For the first five to ten years, I collected verses and thoughts about verses. During that time, I knew I needed to live what I was learning. Living it is significantly more difficult than learning it.

After about ten years of studying about the fear of God, I decided to lead a men's Bible study with the fear of God as the focus. Thoughts from those men opened up many other ideas and insights to understanding the fear of God. I learned different ways to look at the fear of God and discovered more about myself—the way I think and the way I view God and the world. I believe God was opening my eyes slowly to His way and also to my ways.

A few years later, I taught an adult Sunday school class on the fear of God that profoundly affected me. My understanding was, again, expanded. The variety of perspectives and stories that connected to the fear of God showed me that I cannot just do this on my own. It must be done in community. Most exciting was the number of people who came up to me outside of class to tell me they were surprised. They kept seeing the term "fear of the Lord" or "fear of God." I told them God was meeting them and speaking to them. I encouraged them to listen carefully. I was also listening. What stood out the most during that seventeen-week period was how closely God's presence is connected with the fear of God. It's not a run-away-from-God type of fear but rather the no-place-to-go-but-God type of fear. Exodus 20:20 challenged me on these two different fears. "Moses said to the people, 'Do not fear, for God has come to test you, that the fear of him may be before you, that you may not sin.'" But then look at this: "Indeed, so terrifying was the sight that Moses said, 'I tremble with fear'" (Hebrews 12:21). Still, Moses went up the mountain. Israel ran away from God in their fear. Moses moved toward God in his fear. Guess who was blessed?

Those two examples of the presence of God connecting with the fear of God helped me see other scripture that connected them. God revealed example after example throughout the Bible where the fear of God was mentioned. A representation of the presence of God was often mentioned in the context, including prophecy of Jesus's arrival. Immanuel (God with us) is coming.

In the beginning of the Sunday school class, I asked, "What are some of your fears in daily life?" When we discussed those fears, the individuals admitted there was something they wanted to control or were afraid to lose. Some of those people said it had become an idol and was coming between themselves and God. As we looked at many common everyday fears in the Bible, we saw the perceived need to control or something the person was afraid to lose. We found that God often wanted to confront the fears of the people with His presence. Then, instead of creating idols to worship, we would run to God's presence (the fear of God).

One example we didn't talk about at length was Abraham (Abram) lying to protect himself and supposedly Sarah (Sarai) but later being willing to sacrifice Isaac, God's promised heir. It seems that Abraham's faith in God's promise and God's presence took him to that "all in" obedience. "He considered that God was able even to raise him from the dead, from which, figuratively speaking, he did receive him back" (Hebrews 11:19). We found it interesting that once again God's presence, Jesus, was foreshadowed since Jesus truly was the male lamb sacrificed on behalf of Isaac—not only on behalf of Isaac but also on behalf of you and me. I'll discuss this, Lord willing, in an upcoming book on the fear of God.

An example we did talk about in the class was Isaiah 7 and 8. God warned the people of Israel not to fear the kings they thought would attack them but instead trust in God's presence (Immanuel or "God with us") to protect them. This was prophecy of the coming Messiah but also a tangible way to confront their idol of control and their idol of the fear of losing something.

If you think about it, when the fear of God causes us to be unable to run anywhere but into God's presence, that is where God's love is. "There is no fear in love, but perfect love casts out fear. For fear has to do with punishment, and whoever fears has not been perfected in love" (1 John 4:18). When we abide in His presence, we have constant communication with the God who created and sustains everything. We do not have to fear, and we are motivated by love. All that we do can be guided by loving God and then loving others. In other words, we are guided by the wisdom of God who knows all things. Imagine having access to God's mind and asking Him any question and learning what will be best for you and the others around you. Access has been granted in the loving grace of Jesus—Immanuel, God with us.

At the beginning of this chapter, I quoted Paul from 1 Corinthians 2:16, "But we have the mind of Christ." God the Son, who is in constant communication with God the Father and God the Spirit, has brought us into His fellowship. He has restored what was broken all the way back in the Garden of Eden.

Let's go back to Genesis when God walked in the garden in the cool of the day. Adam and Eve had access to Him, as well as to all wisdom and knowledge of the universe for all time and eternity. They had fellowship with Him—communication. God's presence was with them. They had everything they could want except the fruit of the tree of the knowledge of good and evil. "The Lord God took the man and put him in the garden of Eden to work it and keep it. And the Lord God commanded the man, saying, 'You may surely eat of every tree of the garden, but of the tree of the knowledge of good and evil you shall not eat, for in the day that you eat of it you shall surely die'" (Genesis 2:15–17). Then came the first salesman ever—the serpent—who told Eve the very thing she didn't have was the one thing she needed. Was it the fruit? No. That was the instrument, the tangible representation of being like God—being like God so we don't need God anymore. God told Adam, don't eat the fruit, for when you do, you will surely die. Do you remember what Eve saw in the fruit? The tree was good for food, pleasing to the eye, and desirable for gaining wisdom (Genesis 3:6). But God had told Adam that if he ate of it, he would surely die. When Eve and then Adam ate the fruit, did they die? Did Eve get what she wanted? And what did they lose?

Let's look at John 17:3 to start to answer the first question, "Did they die?" In Jesus's prayer to His Father in heaven, He said, "And this is eternal life, that they know you, the only true God, and Jesus Christ whom you have sent" (John 17:3). Eve chose to separate from relationship with God in order to grasp and steal to get wisdom. In that moment, both she and Adam chose to grasp for wisdom in place of relationship with God, and we've been doing that ever since. Remember that Adam and Eve were already like God, created in His image for relationship with Him. "Then God said, 'Let us make man in our image, after our likeness. And let them have dominion over the fish of the sea and over the birds of the heavens and over the livestock and over all the earth and over every creeping thing that creeps on the earth'" (Genesis 1:26). And they had eternal life because they knew God and were known by Him. But all that was lost. What Eve wanted, she already had. However, because of their pride, Adam and Eve both decided on wisdom apart from God. They lost all intimate connection with God who is all wisdom.

Pride and disobedience, better known as sin, was their destruction. "Did God really say?" The way back to life is believing (faith) in the way of truth God provided in Jesus. Yes, it is faith in Jesus found in humbly receiving His salvation through His death and resurrection. Humility brings me back to believing God's Word as He speaks. Pride in me tells me there is a better way. Pride, seeking wisdom apart from God, always leads to death and destruction. Humility, seeking to listen and obey, leads to relationship with Him, knowing Him and the One He sent, Jesus. We ultimately return to wisdom. Paul describes his struggle in his prayer for the Colossians and the Laodiceans, "For I want you to know how great a struggle I have for you and for those at Laodicea and for all who have not seen me face to face, that their hearts may be encouraged, being knit together in love, to reach all the riches of full assurance of understanding and the knowledge of God's mystery, which is Christ, in whom are hidden all the treasures of wisdom and knowledge" (Colossians 2:1–3).

Jesus has always been the access to eternal life. The wisdom we constantly search for and have searched for from the beginning is in Him. Eternal life has always been by faith, and wisdom is the byproduct. The more we, in humility, make ourselves dependent on God in faith and love, the more He takes us into loving each other. The more we love each other, the more we grow in faith together, "that their hearts may be encouraged, being knit together in love, to reach all the riches of full assurance of understanding and the knowledge of God's mystery, which is Christ, in whom are hidden all the treasures of wisdom and knowledge" (Colossians 2:2–3).

We cannot get there by ourselves. As ones who have humbly believed in Jesus's salvation (rescued from death), we become part of His body, and together under Him as head, we more fully and intimately know Him (full riches of complete understanding). That's where humility will lead us—leaning on others and always learning from Jesus, the head, and other believers, His Body. He takes us deeper into His wisdom through which we become more humble, depending on Him and His Body in love more fully. "Who is wise and understanding among you? By his good conduct let him show his works in the meekness of wisdom" (James 3:13).

A typical human question when referring to what God offers is this: "So what's in it for me?" Ah! Thank you for asking that! Here is my favorite passage that answers that question (which I have also asked) in regard to wisdom:

> Then you will understand the fear of the LORD and find the knowledge of God. For the LORD gives wisdom; from his mouth come knowledge and understanding; he stores up sound wisdom for the upright; he is a shield to those who walk in integrity, guarding the paths of justice and watching over the way of his saints. Then you will understand righteousness and justice and equity, every good path; for wisdom will come into your heart, and knowledge will be pleasant to your soul; discretion will watch over you, understanding will guard you, delivering you from the way of evil, from men of perverted speech. (Proverbs 2:5–12)

If we look carefully at this passage, we'll see that it is centered on relationship with God, or more precisely centered in God. "For the LORD gives wisdom" (Proverbs 2:6). Wisdom apart from God leads to death, but in God it leads to life (remember Genesis 3), and again, we are back to John 17:3, "And this is eternal life, that they know you, the only true God, and Jesus Christ whom you have sent." I believe there are many, many—maybe countless—benefits we can receive, but maybe we are asking the wrong question.

What if our search for wisdom asked more accurately, "What's in it for God?" It sounds like we have come full circle to the first chapter of this book. This is precisely what a biblical pursuit of wisdom will do—lead us more fully into the glory of God. When I seek wisdom in a vibrant relationship with Creator God, I am humbled, and He gets the glory. Then, as we discovered in the first chapter, Jesus prays in John 17:22 ("The glory that you have given me I have given to them, that they may be one even as we are one.") that we would be glorified because, it seems, He is glorifying not our work but the Holy Spirit's work within us. I believe this is the humility that comes from wisdom mentioned in

James 3:13. "Who is wise and understanding among you? By his good conduct let him show his works in the meekness of wisdom." God is glorified, and we and others around us receive those benefits.

I once met with a couple who were struggling in their marriage. We had been meeting for a number of sessions when I sensed in my spirit that I was supposed to ask a certain question. I perceived this as the Holy Spirit but did not agree that the question should be asked. I argued that this very question was something that would only cause more conflict and that no good would come out of it. The impression was very strong and incredibly persistent. Finally, I gave in and asked the question. Immediately both of them started talking and then proceeded to argue heatedly. I tried to bring order but decided we would not get anywhere in that session, so I closed in prayer briefly. They left the building very angry with each other.

At our next scheduled meeting, I expected them to call and cancel, but when they arrived, I was shocked. They were holding hands as they walked in, sat down side by side, and couldn't stop looking at each other. I sheepishly asked permission to interrupt so we could start. After praying, I asked them what happened. One of them said, "Remember the question you asked us?" How could I forget? "That was a question we have been avoiding talking about our whole marriage since we knew what would happen. But we needed to deal with it. The argument turned into a deep discussion that opened up so much communication between us. It was the best thing you could have asked." I had to admit it didn't come from me and that I had been convinced I shouldn't ask it. The Holy Spirit knew better.

When we seek wisdom without regard to God and His Word—as we saw Eve and Adam do in Genesis 3—we deny the saving relationship with the Savior along with all access to God who has all wisdom. We miss out on being a vessel of God's glory to bring life to others. Instead, we may get earthly benefits for our heart's desire. Unfortunately, those pursuits are all empty and meaningless and certainly not guaranteed. The teacher and preacher of Ecclesiastes tried it all and got it all, but he said it was all vanity—a vapor, a chasing after the wind.

This all comes back to the first sentence of the first chapter of this book. "I think you know me well enough to know that I want my life to have purpose and meaning." If my life had purpose and meaning and I fully embraced that truth, I would fully believe I was living abundantly. To put it another way, I would fully believe I had lived life to the full. It seems that the teacher of Ecclesiastes was looking for the same thing, just in the wrong places.

    I want to live an abundant life. What might that look like?

Chapter 7

Abundant Living
Living in the fullness of God
necessitates relationship and community.

In the Introduction, I asked you, my dear children, to walk with me on a journey. The goal is to continually walk with Jesus for God's glory. In the process of walking and working out that goal, we abundantly receive God's gift of our hearts' desires. We don't live in mere drudgery just trying to survive until we die. We thrive in peace, joy, and self-control (aka Holy Spirit control). Our entire being increasingly becomes alive, not because of what is taking place but because of Who has taken our place. Our circumstances don't dictate our condition. Our position dictates our destination, and even though on a journey, we have already arrived. As Christ-followers—believers in His salvation for us through His life, death, and resurrection—we are not only with Him but live in Him and He in us.

> I have been crucified with Christ. It is no longer I who live, but Christ who lives in me. And the life I now live in the flesh I live by faith in the Son of God, who loved me and gave himself for me. (Galatians 2:20)
>
> For if we live, we live to the Lord, and if we die, we die to the Lord. So then, whether we live or whether we die, we are the Lord's. (Romans 14:8)
>
> For God has not destined us for wrath, but to obtain salvation through our Lord Jesus Christ, who died for us so that whether we are awake or asleep we might live with him. (1 Thessalonians 5:9–10)

All along this journey of life, we have access to the giver of life through humility of heart, one that cries out for help to Him. He will meet us with His abundant living. We have it, and we are living into it. It is like a coat that is too large for us since we are a child still growing. It keeps us warm, but it is bulky and awkward until we grow into it. When we've worn it long enough, we only notice it when we take it off and feel the cold (or I'm not living abundantly; what happened?) You may ask me, "What is this abundant living that I'm supposed to have and grow into?" Part of it is what we've been exploring in the book so far. It's glory, faith, love, obedience, compassion, wisdom—and I believe an endless supply of other gifts.

When I thought about what aspects abundant living might entail, I came up with four that stood out to me. From my life perspective and also my current life situation, I realize how much more valuable *time* is becoming. For all of us, no matter how old, time is getting shorter. The older we get, life tells us we're running out of time. What if we had all the time we needed to do everything we needed to do? There wouldn't be "I don't have enough time" or "I'm running out of time" or "I'm losing time."

On the other hand, what if we were walking with the Author of time? Wait! That's crazy! But we are. The Almighty God called Himself the I AM (or I was, I am, and I will be). He holds our history, our right now, and our future. Do I believe that? I mean, do I really believe that? That means as Christ-followers, we have the riches of time available to us through Him. Yet on the other hand, we (I know I do) live as if we never have enough time. We think we somehow have the power to control time and the space inside of time. We try to control the future through our fears, anxieties, and worry. All of these require foreseeing the future. Yes, it may be based on past experience, but it is believing that I can anticipate the future. As a result, we try to create contingency plans for every conceivable scenario. I don't know about you, but I try to anticipate those scenarios so my fear doesn't come to pass. I appoint myself god of my future. I might get one scenario in a million correct, but that one will prove to me that my anxiety, my fear, and my worry are completely justified. Therefore, I am god of my future. We call it wise and discerning.

The fruit in the Garden of Eden from the tree of the knowledge of good and evil was also desirable for gaining wisdom. Instead of deeply and intimately pursuing the God of all wisdom in relationship, I try to plan for emergencies. Meanwhile, I'm not sleeping well. I feel tension in my neck, back, and shoulders. I get headaches, and I'm irritable. I start to blame people and get full of negativity. I don't know what you are like when "time" seems to get the best of you. Whether delayed by minutes, hours, days, or years, as I try to control the future, the delay becomes a barrier between God and me. I get angry with the delay and the cause of it. The blame can often go back to God, at least from my perspective. As I have tried to control time and failed, I know that God is truly sovereign, so I often blame Him without even processing it. He could have prevented the delay, but He didn't, so therefore my worry, fear, and anxiety all seem justified.

What if I let Him be the controller of time? These are a few of the results if I trust Him to decide when events should take place and if I talk with Him about my part in those events.

1. My trust in Him grows.
2. My faith in His Word grows.
3. My hope becomes surer; I'm hoping in Him.
4. My prayer (talking with God) becomes more frequent because I want His view.
5. I am more apt to forgive because the past is His to judge and redeem. That person who hurt me will stand before the perfect Judge who always judges justly.
6. In a similar way, my mercy and grace for a person allows God His timing to work in them. I don't have to control the timing of their getting due justice or how much time I give them to change. Do I allow God to change them in His time?
7. I allow God His timing to fulfill His promises when He chooses. If I don't, I can get bitter toward God because I believe He isn't faithful to fulfill His promises in my timetable. He never promised to fulfill them on my timetable—only on His. See Genesis 16 and 21 to

understand how we create so many problems when we try to force God's promises to fit our timetable.
8. Speaking of fulfillment, when we submit all our hopes, plans, expectations, and dreams to our Heavenly Father to decide the right timing, we can be content in the "right now" if we choose to. Even as I write this, God is reminding me of my grumbling about the timing of His ways. If it doesn't meet my expectations, I get annoyed. I have to submit myself to Him and His ways. I don't want to, but I know I really want to want to. So that has become my plea: "Create in me a desire expressed in my actions. I can't get there alone. I need You, God, to work on me."
9. With the great I AM God we serve, He is in all of time at the same time. Because of this, we cannot hide. Lying and deception are currently being exposed in real time at this moment, not some other day. If we believe that, we won't need to be in control of time.

Abundant living when God is King of time doesn't mean we are absolved of all responsibility. Rather, God pulls us gently and sometimes firmly into relationship with Him so we will listen and obey. Humility in this case is submitting ourselves to be directed constantly by our King who is over time. Our relationship with Him becomes sweet and peaceful. We become increasingly content with His way. "So Jesus said to them, 'When you have lifted up the Son of Man, then you will know that I am he, and that I do nothing on my own authority, but speak just as the Father taught me. And he who sent me is with me. He has not left me alone, for I always do the things that are pleasing to him'" (John 8:28–29). "For I have come down from heaven, not to do my own will but the will of him who sent me" (John 6:38).

Abundant living increases as we become whole, fully put together. God's image is allowed to become fully alive in Christ through the power of His Spirit who is alive and at work inside of us by faith. That is *integrity* or wholeness in us. Paul writes:

> But that is not the way you learned Christ!—assuming that you have heard about him and were taught in him, as the truth is in Jesus, to put off your old self, which belongs to your former manner of life and is corrupt through deceitful desires, and to be renewed in the spirit of your minds, and to put on the new self, created after the likeness of God in true righteousness and holiness." (Ephesians 4:20–24)

The more we submit to the Holy Spirit guiding our lives, the more whole we become. We were not designed by God to be independent of Him. As Ephesians 4:24 says, we are "created after the likeness of God in true righteousness and holiness."

The wholeness of abundant living releases us from living in a false reality—one where we twist truth and believe we can create reality where we are superior to God. "If I just twist the truth here, I can appear to be an upstanding Christian while at the same time doing whatever I want or what I think I should want." I have lived this for too much of my life. I created a facade to cover my sin. When I thought the facade could be in danger of cracking, I created another facade to cover that one up. The problem was that I couldn't let anyone deeply into relationship with me because of my fear of being exposed. What if they find out who I really am—a fraud? I will be rejected and therefore lonely. You know what? I was already feeling lonely and rejected because I kept people from getting too close. It wasn't until I was desperate enough for relationship, specifically with my wife, and even before that with God that He broke through my facade, and I asked Him to dismantle it. I confessed—told the truth about who I had been and who I believed myself to be. I repented—I listened to God's truth about me, both broken and healed at the same time. I also needed His work through His Body, the Church (true believers), to help me grow into His image—the image He put in me as part of that Body.

The wholeness I increasingly live into has an effect on my entire body. As my will is submitted to God's Spirit within me, by faith I become more of who I am created to be. My entire being becomes whole, full, and restored. This is the foundation of the Hebrew word *shalom*—wholeness, peace, restoration. Do we wonder why our body, our mind, and our soul are in shambles? Why don't we experience that *shalom*, that wholeness, or as we have been saying, abundant living? We are fragmented. At best, we are having an ongoing conversation with the Holy Spirit, and our general tendency is to follow His prompting out of deep love for our God, creator, and sustainer. More likely we go to church and maybe read the Bible a few times a week. Prayer? A bit.

When the book *Purpose Driven Life* came out, I read it. One of the first questions was this: "How do you view life?" I knew the answer before I finished reading the question. Life is a puzzle. Then I thought about it more and believed that I did really look at it like that. God has the finished work in His hands and in His plan. If I go to Him, who has the full picture (the one on the puzzle box), I can understand how these complicated and confusing pieces of life fit together. I enter more fully into the wholeness of the finished puzzle. Without God, this life is impossible to sort out. Maybe, just maybe, we'll get the edges of the puzzle put together but never see the big picture.

What if we really believe that God is the source of restoring us to wholeness for the display of His splendor? Would we take time to listen to His voice while we plan? Would I ask Him for His desire and His plan for this or that person and then actually pray for them? In that place, I could be content in any circumstance because I would know that God's desire and best for His glory was also for my best. When I am willing to believe that about God, I have an increasing trust that He will work out abundant living in me. As Paul wrote, "Not that I am speaking of being in need, for I have learned in whatever situation I am to be content. I know how to be brought low, and I know how to abound. In any and every circumstance, I have learned the secret of facing plenty and hunger, abundance and need. I can do all things through him who strengthens me" (Philippians 4:11–13).

Again, it comes back to where my reality is grounded. Is it created by me and a compilation of various ideas I have? This reality is heavily influenced by the enemy and culture. Or is my reality increasingly submitted to God's perspective in prayer (conversation with God), interaction with His Word and many other spiritual exercises (disciplines) that assist me in being available to His Spirit? Let's look at some other verses in Philippians.

> Rejoice in the Lord always; again I will say, rejoice. Let your reasonableness be known to everyone. The Lord is at hand; do not be anxious about anything, but in everything by prayer and supplication with thanksgiving let your requests be made known to God. And the peace of God, which surpasses all understanding, will guard your hearts and your minds in Christ Jesus. Finally, brothers, whatever is true, whatever is honorable, whatever is just, whatever is pure, whatever is lovely, whatever is commendable, if there is any excellence, if there is anything worthy of praise, think about these things. What you have learned and received and heard and seen in me—practice these things, and the God of peace will be with you. (Philippians 4:4–9)

We train our minds to believe either our reality or God's reality. On which do you choose to train your mind?

If I train my mind based on my reality, if I base my life on feelings or intellect, my reality is the basis of my choices. Because I can only guess about the future, maybe only an educated guess but a guess nonetheless, I live in fear, anxiety, worry, and stress because living this life was never supposed to be centered on my reality. I have absolutely no control over what happens next.

Look at Philippians 4:4–9 again. Look at where it begins—a choice. Yes, joy is a fruit of the Spirit, a gift given to us. Rejoice is the command to choose joy. Here we are twice told to choose joy, and it is centered on the Lord—always. This shifts both our feelings and our intellect from self-focused toward God-centered. His reality is what we are truly living in. We must by His action of grace in us reorient our hearts and minds in every situation. When we increasingly choose to reorient our hearts and minds to God's presence and His reality through communion with Him in prayer, petition, and thanksgiving, God's peace will guard our minds—*shalom*! There is contentment found in any situation in any circumstance because our reality is in Christ—right now at this moment. Everything else, past and future, is in His hands. There is *no anxiety necessary*! Does that sound easy? At least for me, it isn't easy at all. That's why I have to continually reorient to God's reality and ask Him to do that in me. I believe that abiding or remaining in Him is what allows the fruit of the Spirit to grow by God's grace.

Abundant living flows from the fruit of the Spirit, and the fruit of the Spirit frees us into abundant living. Why? Because all the fruits of the Spirit are fulfilling one of the two greatest commands or both. God has designed us from the very beginning to be most abundantly alive in relationship with Him when two commands are fulfilled in our lives. Love is exactly the fulfillment of both commands that Jesus said were the greatest. "Teacher, which is the great commandment in the Law?' And he said to him, 'You shall love the Lord your God with all your heart and with all your soul and with all your mind. This is the great and first commandment. And a second is like it: You shall love your neighbor as yourself" (Matthew 22:36–39).

Joy, as we said previously, is both a choice and a fruit of the Spirit. I choose to allow God to reorient my mind into rejoicing in His presence. When I get proactive in my relationship with Him and His deep, lavishing love, I find how good His reality is and how He is offering me abundant living no matter in what situation I find myself. Peace is the *shalom* of the Hebrew Bible in abundant living as God designed it to be. Forbearance or patience allows God to be the just Judge He truly is in our lives and in others' lives. This is part of His name or His character. One person hurt me deeply, and I had to consciously and deliberately offer him to God as his righteous Judge. I inherited that sin nature from Adam and Eve who ate the fruit of the tree of the knowledge of good and evil. Because we joined them in their sin, we can never be the righteous judge that God always is. We become free from usurping the role only God is able to fill. Kindness flows from the compassion of God's heart. He proclaimed His name—gracious and compassionate. When we by faith receive His adoption, we take on His name, and the Holy Spirit begins to bear fruit in us. The question is whether we will respond to what the Holy Spirit is doing. "Do not quench the Spirit" (1 Thessalonians 5:19).

The fruit of the Spirit is a barometer of my heart. Am I abiding in the vine who is Jesus? "I am the true vine, and my Father is the vinedresser. I am the vine; you are the branches. Whoever abides in me and I in him, he it is that bears much fruit, for apart from me you can do nothing" (John 15:1, 5). If I find (or others find) that I am not bearing fruit (love, joy, peace, etc.), my attention should *not* be on producing more fruit. I should find out why I am not connected to the Vine. What happened, Lord? What caused me to stop bearing fruit from Jesus? An event? A person? The questions must be addressed to God who knows our heart, not to our own head that has already led us astray. I love the picture of the gardener or vinedresser pruning and picking up a branch, cleaning it and retying it to the trellis. Yes, it is God's work in me. "Therefore, my beloved, as you have always obeyed, so now, not only as in my presence but much more in my absence, work out your own salvation with fear and trembling" (Philippians 2:12). "For this I toil, struggling with all his energy that he powerfully works within me" (Colossians 1:29). This is a matter of faith. Do I believe God can make me stand? "Who are you to pass judgment on the servant of another? It is before his own master that he stands or falls. And he will be upheld, for the Lord is able to make him stand" (Romans 14:4).

This has been a process of growth for me. Even writing this book was a process of growth. I believe God is always able and willing. The real question is whether I am willing. Am I willing to intentionally stay connected to the Vine so His fruit is born in me? Am I willing to do this not just so my life is nicer, more pleasant, or easier but so the character of God is displayed and God is praised? This isn't always, not even often, nice, pleasant, or easy. In fact, we are warned that to be like Christ, our lives will include suffering. This was the Apostle Paul's desire, "that I may know him and the power of his resurrection, and may share his sufferings, becoming like him in his death" (Philippians 3:10). Why? He tells us later "that by any means possible I may attain the resurrection from the dead. Not that I have already obtained this or am already perfect, but I press on to make it my own, because Christ Jesus has made me his own" (Philippians 3:11–12).

Does that seem hard? You may have heard this before: Life is hard, and anyone telling you any differently is selling you something. So what should I do to have that abundant life? I should believe that God does the work as I continuously pursue staying connected to the Vine (Jesus). That takes perseverance.

Chapter 8

Perseverance
In my weakness, I am strong in You, Lord.

Is the condition of our souls the direct result of some level of conscious perseverance? I believe it is, but unto what? In other words, what is our motivation for persevering? I don't know about you, but neither character (Romans 1) nor becoming mature and complete (James 1) were a very good motivator to me most of my life. I didn't want to suffer and endure that suffering just so I could have character or be mature. That didn't make any sense to me when I could just pretend to be mature. I could pretend to have character, skip all the pain and suffering, and everyone would give me accolades and think highly of me. I noticed, though, that I wasn't fulfilled. Don't get me wrong. I enjoyed people thinking I was better than I knew I was. But what was the problem? I knew me, and I was terrified it would all come crashing down if I were revealed, truly revealed.

This verse kept coming back to haunt me (convict is a better word): "The one who speaks on his own authority seeks his own glory; but the one who seeks the glory of him who sent him is true, and in him there is no falsehood" (John 7:18). I knew I wasn't a man of truth, and I did everything I could, including lie to myself, to appear that I was a man of truth. I couldn't keep it going. I wanted more, and I knew I couldn't get there myself. I tried, but the more effort I gave to get into a fulfilling relationship with God seemed to result in more failure and more disappointment, frustration, and discouragement. I was persevering in my reality for my glory. In the end, God will not tolerate that. Oh yes, He is patient and gracious, slow to anger. That's His name. But He is also one "who will by no means clear the guilty" (Exodus 34:7). He desires "that all should reach repentance" (2 Peter 3:9). Why? Because God knows what is best and because He made everything that is not Him, and what is Him is all that is good.

Why wouldn't a good father want what is best for his children? Jesus is very clear about this. "What father among you, if his son asks for a fish, will instead of a fish give him a serpent; or if he asks for an egg, will give him a scorpion? If you then, who are evil, know how to give good gifts to your children, how much more will the heavenly Father give the Holy Spirit to those who ask him!" (Luke 11:11–13). For many years, I maintained my pursuit of God even though I was deceiving myself. Many times I thought I just needed to try harder, do more, read more books, listen to more speakers, read the Bible more, and pray more. I would seem to make a bit of progress, but not a lot was changing. Much of this journey I described in Chapter 3. What you may have seen was that I didn't quit. I have said at various times, "Am I making any progress, Lord?" or "Does anything I do really matter?" Both of those thoughts, especially the second one, drove me deeper into God's Word because I knew He had my answer, and He even had the best questions I needed to be asking.

There were generally four barriers I faced that made it very difficult to persevere, to keep pressing forward until the end. Each has its unique response to persevere. Some come from the outside of me, and some barriers are internal. *Persecution* comes from the outside, if not directly then indirectly. It is an intimidation from the bully we call *the* enemy. *Fatigue* comes from the barrage of resistance we face externally or internally over a period of time, wearing on our resolve. *Apathy* often comes slowly, increasingly discouraging because progress is not apparent. *Fear* is deeply internal and often stems from wounds deep in the past. Let's look at these barriers and possible solutions.

Persecution, depending on its apparent source and intensity, can be somewhat easier to identify and combat with prayer. I have noticed those who are willing to humble themselves before God and before their brothers and sisters in Christ and ask for prayer tend to be more likely to persevere through persecution. Humility always has to include being willing to submit to any change God wants to accomplish in the midst of persecution. But hearing the Holy Spirit identify the barrier as persecution can help us move from discouragement to encouragement. Instead of wondering what might be wrong with me, I start to realize that the enemy is not happy with what God is doing in me. I also find I am much more able to remain joyful in the midst of persecution when people are praying for me, whether I consciously know they are praying or not. This comes across powerfully in Ephesians 6:10–20:

> Finally, be strong in the Lord and in the strength of his might. Put on the whole armor of God, that you may be able to stand against the schemes of the devil. For we do not wrestle against flesh and blood, but against the rulers, against the authorities, against the cosmic powers over this present darkness, against the spiritual forces of evil in the heavenly places. Therefore take up the whole armor of God, that you may be able to withstand in the evil day, and having done all, to stand firm. Stand therefore, having fastened on the belt of truth, and having put on the breastplate of righteousness, and, as shoes for your feet, having put on the readiness given by the gospel of peace. In all circumstances take up the shield of faith, with which you can extinguish all the flaming darts of the evil one; and take the helmet of salvation, and the sword of the Spirit, which is the word of God, praying at all times in the Spirit, with all prayer and supplication. To that end, keep alert with all perseverance, making supplication for all the saints, and also for me, that words may be given to me in opening my mouth boldly to proclaim the mystery of the gospel, for which I am an ambassador in chains, that I may declare it boldly, as I ought to speak.

The Apostle Paul knew persecution personally in many ways, but he spoke of how he persevered. "But though we had already suffered and been shamefully treated at Philippi, as you know, we had boldness in our God to declare to you the gospel of God in the midst of much conflict" (1 Thessalonians 2:2). Why did he have that strength? It was because, as he says in the next verses, there wasn't impurity or an attempt to deceive. If we are in the midst of persecution, we have to check our methods and our motives before God as Paul did. "But just as we have been approved by God to be entrusted with the gospel, so we speak, not to please man, but to please God who tests our hearts. For we never came with words of flattery, as you know, nor with a pretext for greed—God is witness. Nor did we seek glory from people, whether from you or from others, though we could have made demands as apostles of Christ" (1 Thessalonians 2:4–6). In fact, 1 Thessalonians 2 is a good place to go when you believe you are being persecuted.

You are aware that your mom and I faced persecution when we followed God to call out the abuse we heard of and saw. We asked God to reveal truth, and He did. We were threatened, maligned, and slandered, and our names were used as a tool for further abuse. We grieved. We prayed. We asked others to pray. We were separated from many by force but also by the sovereign hand of God. He took what was meant for evil, but He meant it for good as Joseph said in Genesis 50:20. How did we persevere through that? We prayed. We prayed, and we prayed. How did we pray? We quite often asked God if our motives were of Him. At times His answer wasn't clear. Other times, pure motives were intertwined with ungodly ones. Thankfully, God sorted much of that out by His grace. Sometimes He confirmed in our hearts that we were going in the right direction. Other times, Scripture would "randomly" (designed by God) fit the situation. I say randomly, but we fully believe it was the Holy Spirit. Often we were able to hear God's correction in situations that arose, and we chose to yield to His correction. Other times, conversations with others would confirm or correct what we understood. When that was grounded in Scripture, we believed we were going in the right direction. All along the way, we kept asking, "God, if we are going in the wrong direction, speak to us clearly. How do we obey You in the midst of this persecution and persevere if you don't make Your way plain to us?"

Strange, possibly miraculous, circumstances happened during that time. The most memorable was a person who came into a large meeting from a very small, private, exclusive meeting. This person proceeded to talk about what was said in the previous meeting. I was shocked at the information being shared that confirmed what God had already shown us through His Spirit. However, to this day I don't believe that was ever supposed to be repeated outside the exclusive meeting.

Many other events and conversations similarly strengthened and clarified what the Holy Spirit was speaking to our hearts. We had very weak faith, but God by His grace strengthened us. God helped us believe we were hearing from Him, whether confirming or correcting what we believed we heard. This was a time that felt very unstable. Our trust in God was unsteady as was our understanding of reality because of the deception and manipulation. Were we crazy, or was everyone else deceived? It wasn't until most of the direct persecution ended that God connected us with many who had experienced something similar in the same organization. We sought help to heal from the wounds—emotional and spiritual—and even then, the process of healing and forgiving continues.

In the middle of persecution and after the intensity died down, I felt *fatigue*. I was just tired. I wanted to quit working so hard in this life. I wanted something, anything, to fill me up. Those were particularly difficult times for me to persevere. Many I have talked with, men and women alike, begin to ask the question, "What's in it for me?" Perseverance gives way to fatigue (I'm tired of this), which gives way to self-focus (What's in it for me? What do I get out of it?). This fatigue can come during or after persecution, but it also comes before, during, or after a significant spiritual event or a presentation of any kind, especially when we have been doing preparation in our own effort. Fatigue and subsequent self-focus can come after a period of caring and compassion. "I have been giving so much. Now I'm going to focus on *me*!" Fatigue and self-focus also rear their ugly heads when I have given up and given in to sin. Trying to get back to perseverance after self-indulgence feels like I'm tired, and I just can't fight my sinful desires."

Isn't it strange to you? In almost any situation, after it or before it, we are susceptible to fatigue and self-focus. Why? I believe it is because we are made in God's image. Could we say, then, that it's God's fault? By no means! Since the Garden of Eden, we have attempted to usurp God's throne. As I said in the first chapter, we stole the glory for ourselves rather than honoring and glorifying God and letting Him turn and glorify His Spirit who is in us. This was Satan's temptation for Jesus in the wilderness, and it is still his attempt to get us to agree with his coup now: "Take the easy way—avoid hardship, suffering, pain (and in the American culture today—avoid any form of discomfort). We hear it commonly in one of the ads from a famous fast-food restaurant: "You deserve a break today."

What if we went Jesus's way? What if we were truly Jesus-followers in every area of our lives? "Then Jesus told his disciples, 'If anyone would come after me, let him deny himself and take up his cross and follow me. For whoever would save his life will lose it, but whoever loses his life for my sake will find it. For what will it profit a man if he gains the whole world and forfeits his soul? Or what shall a man give in return for his soul?" (Matthew 16:24–26). Jesus's challenge to the disciples came after Peter declared—in his discomfort and fear of losing Jesus and in the midst of a spiritual battle for Jesus to take the easy way out—that Jesus's death shall never happen. Jesus didn't just rebuke Peter; He rebuked Satan. Satan's temptation in the wilderness, his temptation through Peter, and his temptation in the Garden of Gethsemane was to *take the easy way out.*

The book of Hebrews is full of descriptions of Jesus's life and perseverance. Our perseverance begins in the same place it began for Jesus—prayer and submission. "In the days of his flesh, Jesus offered up prayers and supplications, with loud cries and tears, to him who was able to save him from death, and he was heard because of his reverence. Although he was a son, he learned obedience through what he suffered" (Hebrews 5:7–8). Scattered throughout the book of John, Jesus made statements that showed His dependence on God the Father. We have looked at most of these already, but I want to show you again.

> Jesus said to them, "My food is to do the will of him who sent me and to accomplish his work." (John 4:34)

> So Jesus said to them, "Truly, truly, I say to you, the Son can do nothing of his own accord, but only what he sees the Father doing. For whatever the Father does, that the Son does likewise." (John 5:19)

> I can do nothing on my own. As I hear, I judge, and my judgment is just, because I seek not my own will but the will of him who sent me. (John 5:30)

And this is the will of him who sent me, that I should lose nothing of all that he has given me, but raise it up on the last day. (John 6:39)

So Jesus proclaimed, as he taught in the temple, "You know me, and you know where I come from. But I have not come of my own accord. He who sent me is true, and him you do not know." (John 7:28)

So Jesus said to them, "When you have lifted up the Son of Man, then you will know that I am he, and that I do nothing on my own authority, but speak just as the Father taught me. And he who sent me is with me. He has not left me alone, for I always do the things that are pleasing to him." (John 8:28–29)

Do you not believe that I am in the Father and the Father is in me? The words that I say to you I do not speak on my own authority, but the Father who dwells in me does his works. (John 14:10)

How did Jesus depend on His Heavenly Father? What did that look like? Details were omitted for a reason. Maybe our relationship in practical moment-by-moment settings with God looks very situationally specific. We get to pour out whatever is deeply revealed by God's Spirit. Then we get to receive from whatever the Spirit has groaned: "Likewise the Spirit helps us in our weakness. For we do not know what to pray for as we ought, but the Spirit himself intercedes for us with groanings too deep for words. And he who searches hearts knows what is the mind of the Spirit, because the Spirit intercedes for the saints according to the will of God" (Romans 8:26–27). This is the Spirit's intercession for us. We should listen.

When we begin to do this increasingly more consistently, we can find our relationship deepening. I don't know how long it will take. When our listening becomes moment by moment, we get to live in constant awareness of the almighty presence of God, and our heart's desire becomes closer and closer to God's desire. The fullness of God is in the Body of Christ when we as Christ-followers come together to pray (seek God's heart together), share our lives together (listen and rejoice in what God is doing in each person), and search the Scriptures together (explore from many viewpoints God's interaction with His people).

Perseverance is very difficult in the midst of *apathy*. When I didn't have a clear reason to persevere, life was laborious and at times pointless. I lost sight of my hope, my goal, and my purpose. Over time, I focused on maintaining in life instead of being motivated by a purpose outside of myself. Oh, I can be motivated by money, fame, pain, or pleasure, but eventually the emptiness drags me down in a field of mud where every step adds more mud to my feet. There seems no point in the next day, even the next moment. What is my motivation? I don't think it's any coincidence that I just got off the phone with someone who was feeling similarly. He talked about doing what God desired of him, but he didn't feel like he was doing what he had been trained to do. Yet God was changing lives through him. I sensed discontent. I have felt that many, many times in the last seven years. I once found myself scrubbing a swimming pool deck and pool tiles when the pool was closed. I had been a pastor, a missionary, a counselor, a mentor, a teacher, and an administrator, among other titles and jobs. Why, God, was I scrubbing pool tiles on my knees? Every day was agony internally—*I didn't care*! But I wanted to obey.

Almost every day I said out loud to God (because I was all alone in the pool area), "You are wasting my life, God! Why am I doing this? When can I get out?" His answer came after a number of months. "I am taking you to higher studies." "Okay," I responded. "I'll get a doctorate if you want me to." "No," He continued, "in humility." I was oriented to the world's reality—higher studies are more educational degrees. God's orientation meant higher studies in learning to lower myself. I persevered from then on because my motivation changed. I had purpose. Did my apathy go away? No. I battled it daily. Did my attitude change? Yes, increasingly. Was it easier to persevere rather than give up? Absolutely because I knew I was continuing on "unto" something, rather someone else, not just myself. I had a higher purpose coming from God.

Remember the picture I painted for you at the beginning of the chapter on faith about being in the ocean surf with a rock beneath you? This is where the Rock who is our God comes in. When I understand I am or have become apathetic, I need my foot on the Rock to help me stand and get me moving again. What does that mean practically when you are already apathetic? I believe you wouldn't have made it this far in the book if God weren't already melting your apathy. Ask God to continue to be your Rock, and if you doubt, pray this: "I believe; help me out of my unbelief." Choose to do what He says in faith, even when you feel like you can't. Read Ecclesiastes but also Romans 7 and 8. Let Ecclesiastes be a motivator to call out to God to teach you to fear Him. Let Romans 7 show you the place where you are, but look at Romans 8 as God's grace and redemption for you. Then crack open the rest of the Bible, and search for the fear of God or the fear of the Lord. Ask God to shake you out of apathy and into fear of Him.

> For no one can lay a foundation other than that which is laid, which is Jesus Christ. Now if anyone builds on the foundation with gold, silver, precious stones, wood, hay, straw—each one's work will become manifest, for the Day will disclose it, because it will be revealed by fire, and the fire will test what sort of work each one has done. If the work that anyone has built on the foundation survives, he will receive a reward. If anyone's work is burned up, he will suffer loss, though he himself will be saved, but only as through fire. (1 Corinthians 3:11–15)

I said to God many years ago, "I am not interested in Your Word. It is dry and seems like just black ink on white paper. But I know I need Your Word. Please take me to that place where I am interested in Your Word." Soon after that, as a young pastor in a church, I was praying for wisdom to lead. I went to Proverbs, a book on wisdom. I thought it was a good place to go. One of the first verses I saw was Proverbs 9:10, "The fear of the LORD is the beginning of wisdom, and the knowledge of the Holy One is insight." If the fear of the Lord is the beginning of wisdom, I probably should start with the fear of God.

That day I began to look up verses about the fear of God and learned many significant truths over the next twenty-two years. I have studied about, taught on, meditated over, and attempted to live the fear of God, by God's grace. God has answered so significantly that His Word has never been dry again. Many times I have felt distant from God, but His faithful gift of His Word has brought me life, even if my feelings of dryness were still very real. God answered my prayer in the midst of my apathy and gave me a way to press on when I felt like giving up.

For your mom and me, perseverance in faith was especially difficult because of those wounds we experienced and the *fear* growing out of those wounds. We found it extremely difficult to trust fellow believers. We also found God to be more mysterious and maybe even less dependable (at least from a broken heart's perspective). How did we work through that? I believe we are still progressing, but the journey began with honest, heartfelt cries of pain and grief. Yet our honest anger and desire for justice to be served are also offered to God. Our prayer at times is more subdued: "Lord, You led us there, and we trusted You. We often didn't do things Your way, but we tried as often as Your presence was on our mind. No, that's not true. It was as often as we were willing to submit to You. It hurt to have so many dear friends turn their backs on us, especially when we believed very strongly that we were doing Your desire. We are afraid we can't trust hearing You once again, yet we know that is our lifeline."

This was and is part of the fear we developed. In working with many individuals, including some of you, we have found that asking Jesus to identify the depth of the wounds and asking Him to heal those wounds begins to reverse the effects that fear has on us. I believe we might also need to address grief because of the loss involved. What did we lose when that fear began? What pain did that loss cause that was attached to fear? Asking Jesus to meet us in the middle of that grief doesn't change the extent of the pain. We just may not need to carry all of it. Jesus meets us and can take the heavy weight of grief on His shoulders.

Our next question might be, "Jesus what do You want me to do with this fear? It is causing [insert the effects it is having on you—anger, self-protection, self-indulgence, self-defense, etc.]. I don't need that or want that anymore. What do You want to replace it with?" Let Him speak to the depths of the fear in your heart. He may respond with scripture, a hymn, a song, or a mental image of what He is giving you to replace that fear. Listen in your spirit all day long. When and if the fears return, ask Jesus if there is anything more you need to see. Either way, walk through the process again. That may have to happen multiple times a day. The more we bring Jesus into the depths of our fear, the more we acknowledge the presence of the Prince of Peace in our lives.

I believe this process is the difference between fear and the fear of God being active in our life. Fear of the Lord is commanded throughout Scripture. Many have said, "What you fear you worship."[8] We will either try to control our situation because of our fear, or the fear of God will cause us to run back to the loving and faithful rescue of our Savior and the loving arms of our perfect Father. If we become increasingly secure in the fortress of love (God), perseverance will be more consistent. You cannot yield to the desire and temptation to quit, give up, or give in to Satan's lie that says, "God won't save you. He doesn't care. You have to watch out for yourself." Instead, the throne of our gracious and compassionate God Almighty becomes our refuge of peace. Then we can truly live in the confidence of the Apostle Paul.

> For we do not want you to be unaware, brothers, of the affliction we experienced in Asia. For we were so utterly burdened beyond our strength that we despaired of life itself. Indeed, we felt that we had received the sentence of death. But that was to make us rely not on ourselves but on God who raises the dead. He delivered us from such a deadly peril, and he will deliver us. On him we have set our hope that he will deliver us again. You also must help us by prayer, so that many will

---

[8] This will come up in the subsequent book on the fear of God, Lord willing.

give thanks on our behalf for the blessing granted us through the prayers of many. (2 Corinthians 1:8–11)

We put no obstacle in anyone's way, so that no fault may be found with our ministry, but as servants of God we commend ourselves in every way: by great endurance, in afflictions, hardships, calamities, beatings, imprisonments, riots, labors, sleepless nights, hunger; by purity, knowledge, patience, kindness, the Holy Spirit, genuine love; by truthful speech, and the power of God; with the weapons of righteousness for the right hand and for the left; through honor and dishonor, through slander and praise. We are treated as impostors, and yet are true; as unknown, and yet well known; as dying, and behold, we live; as punished, and yet not killed; as sorrowful, yet always rejoicing; as poor, yet making many rich; as having nothing, yet possessing everything. (2 Corinthians 6:3–10)

For though we walk in the flesh, we are not waging war according to the flesh. For the weapons of our warfare are not of the flesh but have divine power to destroy strongholds. We destroy arguments and every lofty opinion raised against the knowledge of God, and take every thought captive to obey Christ. (2 Corinthians 10:3–5)

Paul mostly cared that Jesus was exalted or glorified through His life. "For I know that through your prayers and the help of the Spirit of Jesus Christ this will turn out for my deliverance, as it is my eager expectation and hope that I will not be at all ashamed, but that with full courage now as always Christ will be honored in my body, whether by life or by death. For to me to live is Christ, and to die is gain" (Philippians 1:19–21). We return to where we started this book. Paul, very different than the teacher of Ecclesiastes, found deep and profound meaning in glorifying Jesus as Lord. He knew in the depth of his whole being that there is nothing greater in heaven or earth. We have no greater gift than to live this to the absolute fullest. We will live the fruit of the Spirit without fear and in the security of our identity in Christ. We can live there every day, confident that our lives are priceless, bought with the love of Christ's blood that was shed for us. In response, we can love Him through faith and in obedience.

What will you choose?

Appendix

If you are reading this and you have never acknowledged your need for God and now realize your way is not working—

If you recognize that you cannot get to God by your own effort—

If you need something that is more meaningful—

If you see there is more to life but you aren't sure where that comes from but maybe God can help—

If you are here just because I said to come to the end of the book—

Then:

Get in a place where you can be very honest with yourself and with God out loud. Acknowledge your need for His work, his salvation in your life.

After that:

Jesus, by His life, death, and resurrection made a way for us as sinful humans. Let Him know that you see your sins, and be totally and brutally honest—because He already knows.

Then:

Share your heart with Him if, indeed, you want His salvation for eternity.

I hope this honest and open conversation is a beginning of opening yourself up intentionally to follow Jesus. I also hope you can go back and read this whole book and that Jesus will meet you and transform you. I pray, oh, I pray this will be your way and His way.

Take some time to read the book of John in the Bible. Get connected with people who live like the Jesus you see there. Then read the Psalms, a book of songs, and the rest of the Bible. Carefully read the verses in the Bible—there are many. Live them out in faith and dependence on God.

If you have received His salvation by faith, welcome to the family.

www.ingramcontent.com/pod-product-compliance
Lightning Source LLC
Chambersburg PA
CBHW031654040426
42453CB00006B/302